Bigger and wilder

Life, loss and learning to be a pilgrim

— JILL BAKER —

Sacristy Press

Sacristy Press
PO Box 612, Durham, DH1 9HT

www.sacristy.co.uk

First published in 2023 by Sacristy Press, Durham

Copyright © Jill Baker 2023
The moral rights of the author have been asserted.

All rights reserved, no part of this publication may be reproduced or transmitted in any form or by any means, electronic, mechanical photocopying, documentary, film or in any other format without prior written permission of the publisher.

Scripture quotations, unless otherwise stated, are from the New Revised Standard Version Bible: Anglicized Edition, copyright © 1989, 1995 National Council of the Churches of Christ in the United States of America. Used by permission. All rights reserved worldwide.

Every reasonable effort has been made to trace the copyright holders of material reproduced in this book, but if any have been inadvertently overlooked the publisher would be glad to hear from them.

Sacristy Limited, registered in England & Wales, number 7565667

British Library Cataloguing-in-Publication Data
A catalogue record for the book is available from the British Library

ISBN 978-1-78959-294-8

"For here we have no lasting city, but we are looking for the city that is to come."

Hebrews 13:14

Contents

Preface v
Introduction 1

In the footsteps of saints and scoundrels 7
Chapter 1. Old Testament pilgrims 9
Chapter 2. New Testament pilgrims 22
Chapter 3. Christian pilgrimage: A brief history 30
Chapter 4. Methodism and pilgrimage? 44

Day by day as a pilgrim 63
Chapter 5. Pilgrim graces 65
Chapter 6. Stage 1—Departure 89
Chapter 7. Stage 2—The Pilgrim Path 96
Chapter 8. Stage 3—The Sacred Centre 105
Chapter 9. Stage 4—Endings and beginnings 113

Epilogue: A pilgrimage of grief 120

Appendix: Pilgrimage on the doorstep 135
Pilgrimage resources 147

Preface

As someone with virtually no sense of direction, pilgrimage is not the most obvious sphere of activity for me, but in the years since our son's death by suicide in 2012, pilgrimage has become life-giving for me and at times a lifeline.

Reflecting on Peter's death a few years later I found myself telling someone that his loss had taken me to a place where I needed God to be "bigger and wilder" than I had experienced up until then. Learning something about the ancient spiritual practice of pilgrimage has been a key element of discovering, or rediscovering, God in this way. As I have walked, felt the wind on my face, discovered "thin places", lost my way, found paths, forged paths, sheltered from rain, been alone, been with others, asked questions, read books, listened to the stories of other pilgrims, laughed and wept, God has been there in ways which have sustained me on the often-wearisome, never-ending journey of grief.

What I hope to do in this book is to bring together some of the ancient wisdom of pilgrimage alongside my lived experience, and find through both what I believe pilgrimage has to offer to all of us, whether or not we are able to leave our homes. I conclude by asking myself whether all this pilgrimage wisdom can be a guide through the grief journey which I continue to walk day by day.

I owe a huge debt of gratitude to many people, not all of them mentioned in the text, who have both asked and answered pertinent questions over the past ten years or so. In particular, my thanks go to all those who have taken the risk of coming on pilgrimage with me, who have laughed, lamented and been lost with me, and who have all taught me important life lessons along the way.

Jill Baker
2023

Introduction

A personal perspective

I have written elsewhere about the life and death by suicide of Peter, our younger son, at the age of 18 in July 2012.[1] This book is more about the gift of pilgrimage which was given to me in that bleak time and how that has developed and sustained me over more than a decade.

I hardly need to say that it was the worst time of our lives, nor that our lives have never been the same since. A well-meaning comment made by many people at the time went along the lines of "Your faith will see you through." I found that added to, rather than eased, my burdens, suggesting that I was expected to have or find enough faith to sustain my life in this chasm of grief and dislocation. I clearly remember the Sunday morning when it struck me like a bolt of lightning that it was not my faith which would see me through, but God's grace and only God's grace.

I believe it was God's grace which subsequently led me towards exploring pilgrimage. That journey, appropriately, had a number of mileposts along the way, including further loss:

- November 2012: In response to a suggestion from a friend, Andrew and I spent three days and nights on the Holy Island of Lindisfarne. My friend had described the tiny tidal island as "a healing place", and her words proved true; the light, the calm, the isolation, the bleakness, the quiet, the rhythm, the tides, the ocean, the seals, the beauty of stark winter trees against a darkening sky ... all contributed to a precious break and a longing to return.
- March 2013: My sister-in-law, Cathi, who would not mind, I think, if I described her as "definitely not a walker" and not a regular

---

[1] Jill Baker, *Thanks Peter God* (Derby: Church in the Marketplace, 2016).

church attender either, signed up to join a group of strangers on a pilgrim walk from London to Canterbury and somehow achieved it, collecting prize-winning blisters and much wisdom along the way. I began to wonder how many other women might be interested in some sort of active pilgrimage experience.

- 31 March 2013: At an Easter family lunch, my father-in-law Doug, then aged 78, was asked what he would like to do to celebrate his eightieth birthday. To general surprise (this never having been mentioned before in anyone's memory) he replied by saying that he had always wanted to walk the Camino to Santiago de Compostela. Only weeks later he was diagnosed with terminal cancer and died at the end of that year. Doug didn't reach his special birthday, let alone walk hundreds of miles to mark it.
- July 2013: I completed my term of office as President of Methodist Women in Britain, from which I moved to a year as outgoing Vice-President. My successor, Linda, chose as her theme, "Pilgrims and Companions" and agreed enthusiastically to my suggestion of exploring her theme on the ground by taking groups of women walking—perhaps we realized that it would be helpful to us both if I moved away from the centre of operations!
- August 2013: I led a pilot group of brave and wonderful women on a route which Andrew and I had devised together. We met in Durham, travelled by train to Alnmouth, walked up the east coast and then across the Pilgrim Path to Lindisfarne. More stories from that adventure, and all the ones which followed, feature in the following chapters.
- Meanwhile Cathi, inspired by her achievement on the Canterbury pilgrim trail, began planning to attempt the Camino in Doug's memory. We talked of her coming with me on another walk to Lindisfarne but, tragically, she was diagnosed with pancreatic cancer and died, aged 51, in March 2018.

Perhaps some of this explains my own reluctance to walk the Camino. I know that for many people, "pilgrimage" is synonymous with that most famous and most travelled of ancient routes, and some readers may be disappointed that this book will make virtually no reference to it. At present, the Camino lies outside my own experience, but I am convinced that the pilgrim way of life is open to all—including those who cannot leave their homes. The God who is both bigger and wilder than I had previously realized still beckons us to join the journey which may be inward, outward or both, and to discover discipline and liberation in the pilgrim life.

What is pilgrimage?

"Different things to different people" is probably the only accurate answer to that question, but over the years I have developed my own approach and a simple structure. The working definition with which I begin is to suggest that pilgrimage is *an intentional journey in response to the stirrings of the Spirit.*

I wonder, though, whether even the element of intentionality is essential; or may at times be subconscious, if that is not a contradiction in terms. The decision to set off somewhere can be triggered by many things, and all can be conduits into pilgrimage. Pilgrimage is more than wandering ... but it can start out as wandering. Journeys undertaken with no meaningful purpose can become pilgrimages, perhaps through an exciting discovery on a path which seemed routine—a bit like Moses' encounter with the burning bush.

The first formal pilgrimage I experienced was in 2005 when I joined 90 other members of BBC Radio 4's *Daily Service* audience in a choral pilgrimage following St Paul's second missionary journey through Greece. I heard this advertised on the radio; I had long been fascinated by Paul and keen to visit Greece; I loved choral singing. My parents had been listeners to the *Daily Service* for as long as I could remember, and my father had recently died ... so it was a combination of commemoration, exploration and pure self-indulgence which made me audition and sign up. I don't think I had a single thought in mind that "I need to go on pilgrimage".

It became an incredible adventure with six or seven hours' choral rehearsing every day, and seven broadcasts, some of them live, of both Sunday and weekday worship on Radio 4. The pilgrimage was led by three people whose names are familiar to any regular listeners from those days: Methodist minister Roger Hutchings, Anglican lay woman (now ordained) Clair Jaquiss, and Anglican Canon Stephen Shipley. It was Stephen who, in our final broadcast from Athens, spoke words which have since become almost a rule of life for me:

> Pilgrimage is far more than making a physical journey. It is being prepared to allow that restlessness which is in every human soul to entice us away from our security in search of something deeper, a clearer vision of the God who calls us to his service.[2]

The shape of pilgrimage

I have found it helpful to think of pilgrimage in four stages, to which we return in Chapters 6–9:

- **Departure:** It begins with restlessness, a desire to dig deeper into life, God, self.
- **Journey:** Then comes the pilgrim path, the journeying (which need not be physical), with all its joys and challenges.
- **Encounter:** At some point (or maybe more than one), the pilgrim reaches a "sacred centre", an encounter with otherness.
- **Transformation:** Finally there is a return to be made; hopefully transformed. Yet even in the return is the recognition that the end of every journey is the beginning of the next.

The origins and history of pilgrimage are explored briefly in Part 1, which demonstrates the many and varied ways in which pilgrimage has been regarded over the centuries by the Church, and individuals within the Church. In the Middle Ages, pilgrimage was seen largely as a penitential exercise; thankfully we have moved on from that, but I would want to retain the value of pilgrimage as a spiritual discipline, a way of becoming

---

[2] Words spoken by the Revd Canon Dr Stephen Shipley in the Radio 4 *Daily Service* from Corinth on 23 September 2005. Quoted with permission.

more spiritually formed. Pilgrimage has mystical qualities; it can be about connecting the real (but invisible) internal world of the soul with the outer reality of the body, landscapes, nature and with the God who loves you.

Pilgrimage is undoubtedly also a metaphor for Christian life. This was recognized by John Bunyan as long ago as 1678 when his book *The Pilgrim's Progress* was published, but it is not always recognized today. One of my disappointments over the years in which I have tried to share my enthusiasm for pilgrimage has been when people have said, "I can't be a pilgrim, I don't have enough mobility" (or, even worse, "I don't have enough money"). I hope to get beyond those apparent obstacles in these reflections. Yet many people do think of their lives as a pilgrimage or journey "from cradle to grave", and if that is so, are there particular elements of pilgrimage which can help us make the best of that journey? I think there are.

PART 1

In the footsteps of saints and scoundrels

Turn the pages of the Bible and pilgrims jump out from all sorts of situations. Whilst I would resist the tendency to label every journey as a pilgrimage and every follower as a pilgrim, there are, nevertheless, strong threads of what I would identify as pilgrim ethos and activity throughout our Judeo-Christian heritage. What follows will not be exhaustive; it is rather a selection of some of my favourite pilgrim texts and tales. I begin in the Bible, then race through Christian history without doing justice to any period, before lingering a little longer in my own Methodist tradition and seeing how pilgrimage, whilst often repudiated by Protestants, has real resonance with the faith of the Wesleys and the people called Methodist.

1
Old Testament pilgrims

It is much more difficult to think of an Old Testament character who didn't go on a journey than to list those who did. Was the expulsion of Adam and Eve from the Garden of Eden a pilgrimage? Noah's voyage in the ark almost certainly was, Abram and Sarai's journey to the promised land bears all the hallmarks described above: departure, journey, encounter, transformation. Melchizedek might be seen as an early pilgrim, wandering through Jewish history and intersecting with Abram in a fascinating encounter (Genesis 14:18f.). From many potential candidates I have selected two men and two women whose lives demonstrated facets of pilgrimage.

In the book of Genesis, the two pilgrims I find most fascinating are Rebekah and her son, Jacob. Are these characters saints or scoundrels? Rebekah has an early shining moment but later shows remarkably bad judgement regarding her sons and sets off a cataclysmic chain of events. Jacob has little of the saint about him—but after all, are not "saint" and "scoundrel" two threads present in all of us?

Rebekah (Genesis 24)

The story of Rebekah can be seen as the story of two intertwining pilgrimages, one of an old man, one of a young woman. It begins after the death of Sarah, when Abraham, now aged around 140, decides that Isaac, the son of his old age, the child of the promise, needs a wife if he is indeed to build a great nation. He summons his oldest, most trustworthy servant (almost certainly Eliezer of Damascus, described in Genesis 15:2–3 as having been born in his house) and sends him on a journey to find a bride for Isaac. Marriage with an alien Canaanite is clearly unthinkable; instead a wife is to be sought from among those relatives of Abraham who remained in Mesopotamia. Nor is there any suggestion that Isaac should go on this journey himself; apart from one near brush with death in Chapter 22, Isaac is overprotected throughout his life. The restlessness is Abraham's, but the journey is Eliezer's, a pilgrim path by camel of which we know little until it reaches its "sacred centre" at a well in the city of Nahor, around 400 miles from where he began.

This is the moment for which Eliezer has been preparing and hoping; it is evening, the time when women draw water. The camels kneel and Eliezer makes a pact with God, "Let the girl to whom I shall say, 'Please offer your jar that I may drink', and who shall say 'Drink, and I will water your camels'—let her be the one whom you have appointed for your servant Isaac" (Genesis 24:14). This would be the means by which Eliezer would recognize God's "steadfast love" (as the Hebrew word *hesed*, with all its richness of meaning, is often translated). Before he has finished speaking, Rebekah arrives; she is very fair; she is a virgin; she is ticking boxes faster than she can fill her jar. With great dramatic suspense the servant approaches her, poses the test question ... and she responds with the words he had hoped for; "I will draw water for your camels also, until they have finished drinking" (verse 19). And she does, apparently. Perhaps here we need not worry about the fact that a large thirsty camel can drink up to 200 litres of water a day, and there were ten of them, and Rebekah merely had a jar ...

The next moment is sacred; through its silence it speaks volumes. "The man gazed at her in silence to learn whether or not the LORD had made his journey successful" (verse 21). How vital in the moment of encounter is that silence, that reflection, that pause, assessing what God is saying. Eliezer is clearly satisfied that the Lord has made his journey successful, and he takes out jewellery as a gift, asking whose daughter she may be. Again the answer could not be better: Rebekah is from Abraham's own family; she is Abraham's great-niece (the daughter of Bethuel, son of Milcah, wife of Nahor, Abraham's brother). The family is delighted to offer hospitality to this servant of their kinsman but Eliezer refuses to eat until he has discharged his duty. Her father Bethuel and brother Laban see the hand of God at work at once (and may also have seen the opportunity to have a female member of the family supported by others). When, however, Eliezer is keen to get back on the road, perhaps before anyone changes their mind or his ancient master back in Canaan dies, the family want a delay (verse 56). In what I see as a remarkable verse, amidst the patriarchy of the Middle East in around 2000 BC, the conflict is resolved by Rebekah herself; "'We will call the girl and ask her.' And they called Rebekah and said to her, 'Will you go with this man?' She said, 'I will'" (verses 57–8). So Rebekah and her nurse set off on the road with Eliezer and his men.

As Eliezer prepares for the final stage of his pilgrimage, to return transformed, Rebekah's pilgrimage is about to begin. She has reached the moment of departure; what restlessness, what longings might have lain behind her ready agreement to travel, "I will." What an exemplary pilgrim spirit! With the blessings of her family in her ears she sets off with Eliezer and his men for a 400-mile camel ride, no doubt wondering about Isaac, to whom she is now pledged.

Again little is told of the journey; we pick up the story as they near the camp. It is evening and Isaac is out for a stroll. He sees the camels; Rebekah sees him and veils herself. Then, having received the report of the servant, Isaac takes Rebekah into his mother's tent and "she became his wife; and he loved her" (verse 67). This declaration of love is very rare in the Old Testament narrative, only paralleled in Genesis by the love of Jacob for Rachel (29:18) and the love of Shechem for Dinah (34:3). So Rebekah reaches her sacred centre in the tent of meeting, that encounter with the "other" which will transform the course of her life. Rebekah's horizons have become markedly bigger and wilder.

In Rebekah's story the pilgrim ethos of being ready for anything is boldly demonstrated. Is the whole of our call to follow Jesus summed up in that question, "Will you go with this man?" and our lives shaped by how willingly and how completely we respond, "I will"?

Jacob (Genesis 25–35)

Reading the book of Genesis, we may miss the timescale which lies behind some of the stories. Isaac did not meet and marry Rebekah until he was 40 years old (25:20); by the time his twin sons, Esau and Jacob were born he was 60 (25:26), so Rebekah's prolonged years of barrenness are, for us, two missing decades. We can only imagine the emotions of those years for Rebekah herself. Eventually Jacob bursts onto the scene, gripping the heel of his slightly older brother, Esau.

From the beginning of life, the boys are shown as contrasting characters with Jacob always living up to his name and first appearance as a "grasper". Having bought his brother's birthright with a meal (25:29–34) he goes on, with his mother's help, to trick his now-blind father Isaac into giving him the blessing which should have been Esau's (27:7f.). Such a blessing is a potent end-of-life gift from a father to a son, with a far greater meaning than words or good wishes. In this case it culminates in a prophecy that the recipient will be served by his brother. Given once it cannot be retracted nor given again. No wonder that although Esau appeared to "despise" his birthright in freely exchanging it for food, this time he is all too aware of what has been taken from him, and he is incandescent with rage when the ploy is discovered.

Some time around 1991 in a radio programme I have long since forgotten, the presenter used the phrase, "Every journey is to some extent a flight." Perhaps I remember those words because as a family we were in the process of applying to serve the Methodist Church overseas and I asked myself from what I might be fleeing . . . ? Perhaps from the fear of life passing us by without us noticing, perhaps from a church which seemed to be somewhat clockwork and predictable. Certainly Jacob's pilgrimage begins as a flight from the anger of his brother, who has vowed to kill him. Rebekah sends him north on the long journey she made in the other direction 20 years earlier, to her brother Laban in Haran, planning to recall him once Esau's anger has cooled down. Much more could be said of the wiles of Rebekah, who somehow persuades Isaac that the scheme is his own idea and thereby even secures another blessing for her favourite son (28:1–6).

Is Jacob a pilgrim? Can a journey with such beginnings become a sacred experience? The following chapters suggest it can—as does the testimony of others in every century since Jacob's experience. Pilgrimage can have unlikely origins in which the pilgrim is not so much the intentional seeker as the one sought. Francis Thompson's haunting poem, "The Hound of Heaven" bears this out, as indeed does his own life. Jacob's story has two significant "sacred centres", or encounters with God, one soon after his departure, the other as he, many years later, returns to make peace—or war. In Genesis 28:11, as Jacob settles down to sleep, he little expects his night-time encounter to become a formative incident in his life and indeed in the religious narrative of humanity. His dream of a ladder leading to heaven on which angels ascend and descend, of the Lord appearing to him and promising him the land on which he lies, along with blessing and presence and protection, may seem to our sense of justice to be unlikely consequences of his actions so far. Jacob's own reaction when he awakes is one of surprise, "Surely the LORD is in this place—and I did not know it!" (28:16) and of fear, "How awesome is this place! This is none other than the house of God, and this is the gate of heaven" (28:17). He changes the name of the place to Bethel—the house of God—and it becomes for him, and for others, a place of pilgrimage for the centuries which follow, until it is lost to idolatry under King Jeroboam (1 Kings 12:28–30).

Even after such an extraordinary night, Jacob is still a grasper, he is still making bargains, he is still looking out for himself. Pilgrims are not perfect; they are a mixture of saint and scoundrel, people with faults and failings, in need of grace.

In a reflection of his mother's encounter with Abraham's servant, which led to the meeting of his own parents, Jacob now meets Rachel, the love of his life, at a well. Whereas Rebekah drew water for Eliezer's camels, this time it is Jacob who does the work, drawing water for Rachel's sheep. The match he desires is more complicated than that between Isaac and Rebekah, and ends with Jacob the trickster finding himself on the receiving end of a trick, as Laban ensure that he is married first to Leah, relenting later and allowing him to marry Rachel as well. For some 20 years he serves his uncle, fathering children regularly by Leah and by the sisters' maidservants, Bilhah and Zilpah, until at last Rachel conceives and gives birth to Joseph.

At this point Jacob seems to become restless—now that he has a son by his favourite wife, perhaps he remembers his own mother or his homeland—he asks his father-in-law and employer to send him away (30:25). More trickery follows before Jacob again embarks on a journey (again "to some extent a flight"). The Lord, who has not been mentioned often in the intervening chapters, re-enters the story and encourages Jacob in his plans; "Then the LORD said to Jacob, 'Return to the land of your ancestors and to your kindred, and I will be with you.'" (31:3). Indeed, Jacob relates a dream to his wives in which God, identified as "the God of Bethel, where you anointed a pillar and made a vow to me" (31:13) has told him to depart and head home. Leah and Rachel are happy to throw in their lot with their husband rather than with their father Laban, and the company sets off to the land of Canaan, seemingly with more flocks and herds than are rightfully theirs. Rachel has also stolen the household gods, and the party neglects to tell Laban, who is busy shearing sheep at the time, that they are leaving. We can appreciate Laban's subsequent sense of grievance.

Because of the remote nature of sheep shearing, it is a few days before Laban hears of the departure, and it takes him seven days to catch up with his slippery son-in-law, his two daughters and at least twelve grandchildren (we cannot be sure that Dinah was the only daughter born—it may be that she is named because of the later story about her in Genesis 34 whereas others, as females, are left in obscurity). Once again the narrator makes it clear to us that whatever we feel about Jacob's behaviour (and I confess I cannot take to the man at all), he is somehow favoured by God, for the Lord appears to Laban (Genesis 31:24) with the instruction, "Take heed that you say not a word to Jacob, either good or bad."

We may therefore imagine Laban speaking through gritted teeth in the following verses as, when they meet in the hill country of Gilead, he remonstrates with Jacob in as polite a manner as he can muster. The theft of the household gods by Rachel is an added complication, as Jacob is ignorant of that, and Rachel's deceit allows Jacob an unwarranted display of self-righteous anger, but eventually all is resolved between the men.

A covenant is made and the two companies part, Laban returning home and Jacob continuing along the pilgrim path.

With the potential enemy and risk of Laban behind him, Jacob's thoughts turn to the potential enemy and risk ahead: his wronged brother Esau. He sends messengers to Esau with gifts of animals and slaves, but the messengers return with the unnerving news that Esau is on his way to meet his brother, along with 400 men. Jacob fears the worst and organizes damage limitation, dividing the people and possessions with which he is travelling into two companies, hoping that one at least might be able to escape if Esau attacks. He sends further generous gifts of animals, instructing the servants to give them in his name to Esau. He also prays fervently, reminding God that this is all a divine idea and it is therefore necessary for God to keep Jacob alive to fulfil it (32:9-12).

Now comes Jacob's second "sacred centre", another nocturnal experience. After sending his closest family across the ford of Jabbok, Jacob is alone, and a man comes and wrestles with him throughout the night (32:24). It is a dark, mysterious story with at least three significant outcomes, all of which have something to say about the nature of pilgrimage:

- Jacob wrestles with a man/with God. Pilgrimage can be a time to allow our wrestlings with God to come to the surface and be acknowledged, to be faced and perhaps, as for Jacob, worked through. The story suggests that God is not averse to opposition or even being prevailed against. This is the God who centuries later does not despise the cross.
- Jacob's hip is dislocated. Wholeness takes many forms. As Jacob limps into the sunrise after this encounter he is, perhaps, more whole than ever before. Pilgrimage is not a walk in the park, it is often demanding.
- Jacob's name is changed to Israel. Pilgrimage is transformative and can change the direction of our journey and the nature of our quest. The name change is reinforced in 35:10.

Having said that, I still don't warm to the way Jacob continues through life, but perhaps that is what I need Jacob to teach me... that grace is not just for people I like, or people like me . . . grace is for everyone. Chapter 33 is heart-warming—the brothers meet and embrace, as brothers are meant to do (elder brother in Luke 15 take note—you were supposed to be the one embracing the prodigal and throwing the robe around him, not your father). Tellingly, however, the brothers realize that living cheek by jowl might not be a happy-ever-after ending and they separate again; Esau returns to Seir and Jacob goes on to Succoth and then to Shechem. Their only further recorded meeting is to bury their father, Isaac, together (he, surprisingly, having been on the point of death 40 years before, has now lived to be 180).

Jacob does, however, return to Bethel (Chapter 35). His piety and morality have begun to weaken in Shechem and so, at God's direction he cleans up his act, leaves the foreign gods behind and settles near to the place of his dream. It seems that God is with him in such a way that those around are terrified and no one gives chase. But here, back in Bethel, we learn that Deborah, Rebekah's nurse, dies and is buried under an oak (verse 8). Whether this is the same nurse who left Haran with Rebekah in 24:59 we cannot be sure, as the nurse is not named at that point and has not been mentioned since. If so, how does she come to be with Jacob now? It seems unlikely that she has accompanied Jacob through all his intervening adventures—where was she when he lay down alone to dream of a ladder? I prefer to think that she came with Esau to meet her mistress's favourite son once again and chose to stay with him. Who knows? But here she dies and here she is buried.

This chapter also records the birth of Rachel's second son, Benjamin, (verse 18) to complete the 12 sons needed to head up the tribes of Israel. Rachel herself dies in childbirth, not far from Bethlehem. Jacob's pilgrim wanderings come full circle as he is reunited with his father Isaac at Hebron, "where Abraham and Isaac had resided as aliens", and the death of Isaac rounds off the Jacob narratives. There is often something cyclical about pilgrimage, for the end of every journey is the beginning of the next.

Moses (Exodus 1–3)

As we move into Exodus, we find the towering figure of Moses, who seems to be an archetype of almost everything... so why not also of a pilgrim? Looking at his life through the lens of the four stages mentioned in the introduction and developed in Chapters 6 to 9, Moses fits the bill, and in doing so displays many of the pilgrim attitudes to which we return in Chapter 5.

Departure: Born to a brave and resourceful Hebrew woman yet brought up in the home of an Egyptian princess, Moses would have every reason to be confused about where his loyalties lie and to be restless as a result. Somehow, he seems to know very well that he is a Hebrew and despite his bread being buttered by Egypt he has the courage to stand up to the oppression of the Egyptians against his people. This leads him to commit murder and to flee into the desert. For him, the idea that "every journey is, to some extent, a flight" is evident.

Journey: Travelling in the liminal space "beyond the wilderness", Moses demonstrates his attentiveness as he notices a bush which is on fire without being consumed. In my own life, I return again and again to his little phrase, "I will turn aside and see..." for attentiveness is a central thread of pilgrimage. Pilgrims are not so tied to the clock or to the map that they cannot "turn aside and see" what might be to one side of the path or the other. I feel sure that the burning bush was not immediately in front of Moses but that he needed to divert from his path to see it. How often, I wonder, have I pursued a goal with such intensity that I may have missed bushes bursting into flame to my left or to my right?

Encounter: Moses' attentiveness is rewarded as he hears the voice of God. He discovers that he is on holy ground, he removes his shoes and encounters God. He enters into conversation with the divine presence, who, after Moses' questioning, reveals his sacred name and nature to Moses in a few words, the translation and meaning of which have continued to fascinate and test scholars ever since: YHWH, the Tetragrammaton, "I am who I am" or "I will be who I will be" or even, perhaps, just "I am"—a phrase well known from John's Gospel.

Transformation: Moses' mission is to set the people of God free, to move with them into another pilgrimage journey, through the wilderness to the promised land. But first he must return to Pharaoh, not as a helpless baby in need of protection, nor as a member of an oppressed minority, but as a revolutionary, a challenger, an emissary from the living God. Moses doesn't slip easily into this role and the series of extenuating circumstances which he presents one by one to God may remind some of us of our own reluctance at times to pick up the pilgrim's staff and go where God sends us. The call to journey is often a reckless, dangerous call, for it is the call of a big and wild God. We know, like Moses, that we will never be the same; we recognize, like Moses, that the end of one journey is so often the beginning of the next.

Ruth

In their different ways, many of the characters in the story of Ruth are pilgrims:

- Elimelech, who sets off on a journey into enemy territory to try and save his family from famine, only to die there and leave them unprotected.
- Orpah, who begins a journey to a foreign land but feels the call to turn back and remain with the familiar—that too can be the way in which pilgrimage works out.
- Naomi, who travels not only physically but also emotionally, from fullness to emptiness and back to fullness, as she holds in her arms the infant Obed with all the associations of his ancestry and descendants.
- Even Boaz, who doesn't travel many miles in the narrative, goes on a journey of relationship and human involvement.
- But it is Ruth, the eponymous heroine of the story, whose pilgrimage is the most gripping.

Ruth, the Moabitess, was not brought up in the faith of Yahweh, but married into an immigrant Jewish family which had set up home in her land. Was there a stigma attached to that? We know that Israel hated Moab; was the hostility reciprocated? Perhaps her neighbours felt she had received her just desserts when her husband died without fathering a child. Elimelech, Mahlon and Chilion all die, and so this little household is formed—three women unrelated by blood, crossing boundaries of race and culture, united in widowhood and vulnerability. When Naomi hears that there is once again food in Bethlehem, they set off together. Do Ruth and Orpah reflect as they make their decision to depart, that this time it will be they who are the foreigners?

The journey was approximately 50 miles, over quite rugged terrain. Naomi had made the journey in the opposite direction ten years earlier. As she returns, she must surely have reflected on how her life has changed since then. Instead of being accompanied by three men to whom she could look for support, protection and provision, she now has with her two foreign women who may expect her to provide them with new husbands. Does she wonder how her old friends will view her if she arrives back in Bethlehem with two Moabite women? Will she be the object of scorn for allowing her sons to marry outside the faith? How will people treat Ruth and Orpah? Will anyone consider marrying these Moabite widows? No wonder she pauses on the way (Ruth 1:8f.).

In a well-known and much-loved passage from Chapter 1, Naomi encourages her daughters-in-law to return to their families and find new husbands in Moab. Initially both refuse, but Naomi is insistent and points out the improbability of her being able to provide them with new husbands. Amidst tears and loud weeping Orpah decides to return, but Ruth "clung" to Naomi and utters a pledge of love, loyalty and even of conversion:

> Do not press me to leave you or to turn back from following you!
> Where you go, I will go; where you lodge, I will lodge;
> your people shall be my people, and your God my God.
> Where you die, I will die— there will I be buried.
> May the LORD do thus and so to me, and more as well, if
>   even death parts me from you! (Ruth 1:16–17)

Naomi has nothing to say in return—is she, perhaps, a little choked by the emotion of the moment?—and they continue to Bethlehem. It is a wonderful pilgrim moment. A little like Rebekah before her, Ruth makes up her own mind about the choices facing her and decides to risk a journey into the unknown. What did Ruth know of the two worlds between which she was choosing? The narrator gives us as readers a hint about how this will all turn out; they are returning to Bethlehem "at the beginning of the barley harvest" (1:22) so we may expect this story of famine to turn into a story of feasting and for all to end well for Ruth. Ruth herself knows nothing of that when she makes her choice to follow the pilgrim path. Reading on through the complexities of ancient Israelite law, Naomi's wiles and Ruth's hard work and courage, we see how the pilgrimage leads to an encounter amongst heaps of grain at a threshing-floor and to the birth of a child.

When, in 2:10, Ruth questions the kindness being shown to her by Boaz (as well she might—she is in a vulnerable position and might easily lose what little reputation she has if she becomes entangled with a powerful man who has every opportunity to exploit her), the book's author gives to Boaz a speech which indicates how the story's readers (of any generation) are to regard this foreign woman:

> All that you have done for your mother-in-law since the death of your husband has been fully told me, and how you left your father and mother and your native land and came to a people that you did not know before. May the LORD reward you for your deeds, and may you have a full reward from the LORD, the God of Israel, under whose wings you have come for refuge! (2:11–12)

Ruth's economic position and her religious status are both transformed, and her name is lodged forever in the family tree of salvation. Through these and many other characters, the pilgrim spirit is alive and well in the narrative of the Bible.

After moving to Glasgow in 2015, I began researching pilgrim routes in Scotland and explored the Church of Scotland Cathedral dedicated to the city's founder, St Mungo, as a possible starting point. There, in the tiled floor of the underground sacristy, I was delighted to discover five Bible texts, all of which can be related to the journey of life and to pilgrimage, tiny snippets which point to the bigger and wilder journey of God's relationship with humankind:

- Hold up my goings in thy paths that my footsteps slip not. Psalm 17:5 (KJV)
- Let us run with patience the race that is set before us. Hebrews 12:1 (KJV)
- He that walketh uprightly walketh surely. Proverbs 10:9 (KJV)
- Ponder the path of thy feet and let all thy ways be established. Proverbs 4:26 (KJV)
- To guide our feet into the way of peace. Luke 1:79 (KJV)

All this might tempt me to claim that pilgrimage is a biblical imperative!

2

New Testament pilgrims

We could approach the New Testament in a similar way and find women and men whose stories are stories of journey and pilgrimage. Jesus himself may be seen as a pilgrim, and each of the four Gospels is, in its own way, a pilgrim tale. Paul would clearly be a contender—making for a long book! The Acts of the Apostles is a complex web of interwoven journeys which together chart the pilgrimage of the early church. Instead of untangling it, let's take a closer look at a few words or phrases which point us to the pilgrim spirit in the New Testament.

Perigrinatus

The word "pilgrim" is widely believed to have its roots in the Latin word *peregrinus*, a combination of *per* (through) and *ager* (field, country or land). From here the word travelled into Middle English as something like *pilegrim* and so today to the word with which we are familiar.

The verse: "Then his mother and his brothers came to him, but they could not reach him because of the crowd" (Luke 8:19) is usually translated into English as above, using standard verbs such as "came" to describe the journeying of Mary and her sons. Interestingly however, the Church Father Tertullian (AD 155–240) uses the Latin word *perigrinatus* at this point, effectively calling Mary a pilgrim. Looking back into the Greek text of this chapter, we see why Tertullian may have chosen to do so: the Greek word used is *paregeneto*, a less common word which (used also by Matthew in his description of the journeying of the magi and in a few other places[3]) might suggest something more akin to *perigrinatus*.

Perhaps this is significant, perhaps it is not, but I rather like the idea of Mary, the mother of Jesus, as the first Christian pilgrim, travelling around to see and hear Jesus in his own journeying. After all, Mary has already made important journeys in her life; from Nazareth in Galilee to the Judean hill country to spend time with Elizabeth (Luke 1:39-40), from Nazareth to Bethlehem for the census and subsequent birth of Jesus (Luke 2:4-6), to Jerusalem for Jesus to be dedicated (Luke 2:22), back to Galilee (Luke 2:39), to Jerusalem each year for the Passover (Luke 2:41) and, in Matthew's birth narratives, into Egypt for his protection (Matthew 2:13-15). Mary was clearly willing to travel and many of the qualities she demonstrates in her life are amongst the pilgrim attitudes which we shall examine in Chapter 5.

Exodus

The Greek name for the second book of the Hebrew Scriptures, "Exodus", translates as departure or "way out", coming from two small Greek words, *ex* (out) and *odos* (way or road). You can find this same word indicating exits in public buildings in Greece today. As the name of a book of the Bible, it refers to the travels (pilgrimage?) of the Israelite nation after escaping slavery in Egypt and before entering the promised land, Canaan.

Luke picks up this word in his telling of the transfiguration of Jesus in Chapter 9 (28-40). In verse 31 we read, "They appeared in glory and were speaking of his departure, which he was about to accomplish at Jerusalem." The word used for departure is *exodos* (exodus). Again, we can't be sure how significant this is, but we do know that Luke is a skilled

---

[3] Luke 8:19 GRK: *Paregeneto de pros* came to him; Luke 11:6 GRK: *philos mou paregeneto ex odou* a friend of mine has come to me from a journey; Luke 19:16 GRK: *paregeneto de o* The first appeared, saying, Master; John 8:2 GRK: *de palin paregeneto eis to* Early in the morning He came again; 2 Timothy 4:16 GRK: *oudeis moi paregeneto alla pantes* no one supported me, but all/no one me stood with but all.

writer who, throughout his two New Testament volumes, the Gospel of Luke and the Acts of the Apostles, chooses and uses words carefully and meaningfully. So we might be allowed to imagine that Luke is deliberately comparing the "departure" Jesus is about to make through his death on a wooden cross to the departure made centuries earlier by the Hebrew people after blood on their wooden doorposts saved them from the angel of death (Exodus 12:7).

Like the fruit around a precious seed, the whole story of the transfiguration which surrounds that single, telling word, "exodus", can be a paradigm for pilgrimage. The fishermen Peter, John and James depart from their usual habitation at sea level and make a strenuous and possibly somewhat scary journey up a mountain (mountaineering was not a sport amongst first-century Jews who would have held onto the Old Testament understanding of mountains as dangerous places inhabited by wild beasts). These men were strong but had probably had little opportunity to develop the particular muscles needed for ascent, and Luke tells us they were weighed down with sleep by the time they stopped. Here on the mountain, amidst their longing for rest, they experience a dramatic encounter as Jesus is transfigured before them and they glimpse Moses and Elijah too. Like many of us at such high points, they want to cling to the moment, but all too quickly it is over and they have to return, but they have certainly been transformed by their experience. They come down to earth with its demands and difficulties. The end of one journey is the beginning of the next.

On the road

The wonderful Easter Sunday evening story of the travellers on the Emmaus Road (Luke 24:13–35) is a favourite with me as with many. The narrative is brilliantly paced, entering into the initial grief of Cleopas and his companion then gently drawing back the veil, verse by verse, until the burst of energy which is recognition, resurrection and return. It is undoubtedly a pilgrim story and demonstrates without any forcing the four-fold nature of pilgrimage, mentioned in the introduction and further developed in Chapters 6 to 9:

- **Departure:** On the first day of the week (Sunday), the pilgrims, Cleopas and an unnamed companion, often thought to have been his wife, set off from Jerusalem, the centre of high drama over the past few days, and the site of the crucifixion of Jesus on the previous Friday.
- **Journey:** We are given a close account of their journey to Emmaus, of the unknown traveller who draws alongside, of the conversation on the way until they reach their home and press hospitality upon him.
- **Encounter:** As their guest takes the bread in his hands, blesses it, breaks it and gives it to them, their eyes are opened and they recognize him, even as he vanishes from their sight. What a moment!
- **Transformation:** Weary as they may have seemed earlier on, they are renewed and re-energized by this encounter and they return to Jerusalem, a walk of around seven miles, to share their good news.

Within this beautifully told story I take note of the little Greek phrase *en te odo* (on the road), which is where the main part of the narrative takes place. We have noted above that *odos* is a common word for way or road, and it is used frequently in the New Testament. Cleopas and his companion note how their hearts burned within them "while he was talking to us on the road, while he was opening the scriptures to us". For a pilgrim, so much is discovered "on the road", by getting moving, by engaging in conversation (or in silence), by allowing the physical rhythm of walking to take the mind and spirit to new places and discoveries.

"The Way" becomes the first description of the new lives of Jesus' followers. Before they were called "Christians" at Antioch (Acts 11:26) Saul asks for letters from the high priest in Jerusalem to the synagogues at Damascus "so that if he found any who belonged to the Way, men or women, he might bring them bound to Jerusalem" (Acts 9:2). Again, Luke captures something of the lovely irony that it is as Saul makes his own way along the road to Damascus in pursuit of this goal that he experiences a "sacred centre" moment and is never the same again. The heart of being Christ's disciple is about journey—following him in the way, *en te odo*.

In Acts 8, we meet another figure "in the way" or on the road, the Ethiopian official who has been worshipping in Jerusalem and is now returning home by chariot, reading aloud from the prophet Isaiah as he goes. The Holy Spirit sends Philip to meet him and help him to understand the passage he is reading (surely not a random choice for a man described as a eunuch, as he seeks truth from Isaiah 53:7 about how someone who has faced the knife and been robbed of heir or posterity might still be acceptable to God). Along the way (*kata ten odon*), they find water for the official to be baptized, and in verse 39 he goes "on his way" (*odou autou*) rejoicing.

It is an ordinary word, used hundreds of times in the New Testament as we might expect. But it is also a word which can define our Christian discipleship and keep us moving as individual followers of Jesus and as a "discipleship movement shaped for mission", a phrase used widely by the Methodist Church in Britain over the past decade. More recently the Methodist Church has put resources into developing *A Methodist Way of Life*.[4]

Seeking (Hebrews 13:14)

Since my teenage years, I have been captivated by the book of Hebrews. When I was about 17, I thought I understood it; now I'm not so sure! It is a book of many layers, written to appeal to a somewhat different readership from much of the New Testament, and probably could be seen as the "Middle-Earth" epistle. The writer—whoever they were—draws the reader into parallel worlds which shadow and fulfil each other. We are encouraged to understand that what can be seen and touched is not as important as what cannot be handled, and so to make the journey from trusting in the practices and structures of the Jewish faith to an acceptance of Christ as the fulfilment of that religious system and as the "pioneer and perfecter of our faith" (12:2).

---

[4] <https://www.methodist.org.uk/our-faith/a-methodist-way-of-life/>, accessed 8 February 2023.

As the complex reasoning of the book moves into more reflective prose about faith in Chapter 11, we find many of our Sunday school heroes mentioned (alongside others of whom we may never have heard). The writer describes these great men and women of the faith in this way:

> All of these died in faith without having received the promises, but from a distance they saw and greeted them. They confessed that they were strangers and foreigners on the earth, for people who speak in this way make it clear that they are seeking a homeland. If they had been thinking of the land that they had left behind, they would have had opportunity to return. But as it is, they desire a better country, that is, a heavenly one. Therefore God is not ashamed to be called their God; indeed, he has prepared a city for them (Hebrews 11:13-16).

It could be a textbook description of pilgrims and is, for me, a defining text. "They are seeking" in verse 14 uses the Greek word *epizētousin*, my final pilgrim word from the New Testament (for now). The word is strong—"seeking after", "searching for", even "craving"—and is picked up again a little later in Chapter 13.

Before that we have the beautiful opening of Chapter 12; verses 1-4 along with verses 12-13 offer us more words to inspire any pilgrim, or long-distance walker, or marathon runner and give the full context for one of the pilgrim texts from St Mungo's Cathedral:

> Therefore, since we are surrounded by so great a cloud of witnesses, let us also lay aside every weight and the sin that clings so closely, and let us run with perseverance the race that is set before us, looking to Jesus the pioneer and perfecter of our faith, who for the sake of the joy that was set before him endured the cross, disregarding its shame, and has taken his seat at the right hand of the throne of God. Consider him who endured such hostility against himself from sinners, so that you may not grow weary or lose heart. In your struggle against sin you have not yet resisted to the point of shedding your blood...

> Therefore lift your drooping hands and strengthen your weak knees, and make straight paths for your feet, so that what is lame may not be put out of joint, but rather be healed (Hebrews 12:1-4,12-13).

And then, in Chapter 13, the writer brings full circle these musings on the Christian journey and seals them with a repetition of the same Greek verb, *epizētoumen*. After some reminders about the efficacy of grace over law, the writer points outside the camp to Jesus who suffered "outside the city gate" and, having brought us back to think about a city (as mentioned in 11:16) goes on to write: "For here we have no lasting city, but we are looking for the city that is to come" (13:14). Different translations of the verse add different shades of meaning, but the key word, translated here as "looking" is a powerful Greek one, all of whose ten or so uses (in various forms) in the New Testament are evocative and urgent.[5] Seeking is another vital strand of pilgrimage.

This mention of "the city that is to come" as the final destination for all pilgrimage leads me down a short diversion about the significance for pilgrimage of cities as well as rural idylls. Jerusalem, of course; Rome has a long association with pilgrimage (albeit the place where I managed to lose two women on a bus and three in the underground . . . but all were eventually restored to the group!). Any city will contain features worthy of discovery by a pilgrim, not least the city where I now live, Glasgow. Although living in Slough in 2014, when Glasgow hosted the Commonwealth Games, I became involved in the movement of prayer for that event and daily for 100 days used the city's motto as part of my prayer; "Let Glasgow flourish by the preaching of his word and the praising of his name". It was a thrill to arrive in Glasgow to live and to see those words (admittedly more usually abbreviated now to "Let Glasgow flourish") all around the city and realize that I had a part to play in this prayer myself. Since then, exploring Glasgow and sharing it with others has led to moments of encounter and transformation, through

---

[5] *epizētoumen* and variants found in Matthew 6:32; 12:39; 16:4; Luke 4:42; 12:30; Acts 12:19; 13:7; 19:39; Romans 11:7; Philippians 4:17; Hebrews 11:14.

the stories behind the architecture and history, or in encounters with the art and culture of the city; Salvador Dali's *Christ of St John of the Cross* in Kelvingrove Art Gallery and Museum is a focus of pilgrimage for many with, most days, a small queue waiting to enter the booth where it is displayed.

For John Bunyan, imprisoned in Bedfordshire County jail in the latter part of the seventeenth century, it was a vision of the Celestial City, which formed the climax of his great work *The Pilgrim's Progress from This World to That Which Is to Come* (to which we make further reference in the next chapter). Surely Hebrews 13:14 played its part in Bunyan's inspiration; as it certainly did for Johannes Brahms around 200 years later, when he set the German text of this verse in the extraordinary sixth movement of *A German Requiem*. It was through Brahms' setting that I learned to pay attention to these words, when, as a new and struggling-to-sight-read-well-enough member of the Durham University Choral Society in 1979, I was for the first time exposed to this magnificent piece of German choral music. Set in the key of C minor, the movement is haunting but insistent: you have to seek, you have to follow, you have to find that city which is to come. It became the first classical record I bought (in the first vinyl era) and is still one to which I listen more than most. If you haven't heard "Denn wir haben hie keine bleibende Statt", you could come to my funeral when I hope someone will remember that this is the piece of music to which I want to make my departure from this world, ready for whatever pilgrimage begins as this one ends. Or you could probably find a recording closer to home.

3

Christian pilgrimage: A brief history

Pilgrimages need starting points. As a starting point for the whole Christian story, I would propose the annunciation in Nazareth. As the angel Gabriel visits Mary and announces that she will bear a child who is to be God's Son, the seeds are sown of all that will follow. So it feels appropriate to locate the starting point of Christian pilgrimage with Mary too, especially bearing in mind her attempt to follow Jesus in Luke 8:19.

However, for an idea or a practice to be recognized and given a name takes time and it is impossible to say exactly when the Christian faith first identified "pilgrimage". What follows here is a collection of snippets from history about the emergence of pilgrimage. It is not comprehensive, but, like the famous shell signs on the Camino to Santiago de Compostela, it may provide enough direction to navigate a path through the centuries. It employs a varied and perhaps unlikely cast: it features a second-century martyr; then, as we move into the fourth century, an empress, a translator, an unnamed French man, a bishop and a wealthy Spanish woman—a veritable pilgrim band in their own right!

The martyr: Polycarp

Christian pilgrimage has origins in martyrdom. The first Christian after New Testament times whose martyrdom is chronicled is thought to be Polycarp, Bishop of Smyrna, who died perhaps as early as AD 156. In *The Martyrdom of Polycarp*, written in the form of a letter to churches, probably in the latter part of the second century, the unknown author refers thus to Polycarp's remains:

Later, we collected up his bones, more precious than jewels and better purified than gold, and put them in an appropriate place where, the Lord willing, we shall celebrate the birthday of his martyrdom each year with joy and rejoicing, both to remember those who have run their race and to prepare those yet to walk in their steps.

There was a sense even from early days that the sites of such martyrdom, or the location of the relics of martyrs and apostles, were places where heaven and earth met, not unlike the "thin places" of which contemporary spirituality often speaks.

The Empress: Helena

Helena Augusta, mother of Constantine the Great who was Roman Emperor from AD 306–37, can be given considerable credit for laying the foundations of pilgrimage. Aided in her quest to locate the relics of the Christian religion by the resources of the empire (to which her son gave her unlimited access) she travelled to Palestine in AD 326–8. The church historian Eusebius wrote in detail about this and other visits and, as a result, Helena is linked to several pilgrim sites in the Middle East, most famously the Church of the Nativity in Bethlehem and the Church of the Holy Sepulchre in Jerusalem, which mark the birth and the death of Jesus. Eusebius records that in Jerusalem during the 130s the Emperor Hadrian had built a temple to Venus over the supposed site of Calvary. Helena had the temple to Venus destroyed and legend suggests that excavation discovered three wooden crosses at the site. The miraculous healing of a dying woman further proved one of them to be the "True Cross". This gave Constantine the assurance he required, and he ordered the building of the Church of the Holy Sepulchre, probably under the supervision of Bishop Macarius of Jerusalem. The veracity both of the legends and the locations is still debated, but Helena's standing as an early pilgrim and Eusebius' reliable reporting of events lends weight to their conclusions. Helena is associated with other sites and relics, many of which are still on display in museums in Cyprus and Rome.

A thirteenth-century map of Jerusalem shows it as the meeting place of three continents, Asia, Africa and Europe. Its current position, somewhat sensitive and precarious, is as the meeting place of three world faiths; Jewish pilgrims travel to their most sacred site, the Western Wall of the Temple; Muslims see the Dome of the Rock, *al-Haram al-Sharif* (or the Al-Aqsa Compound) as their third most significant pilgrim site (after Mecca and Medina); and Christians journey to the city and to neighbouring Bethlehem to see the locations of the birth and death of Jesus.

In these stories, as in so many stories, faith and politics are intertwined and almost every statement of fact must be qualified and considered alongside conflicting evidence. Whether Constantine was converted to Christianity in AD 312 or on his deathbed in 337; which kind of Christianity he subscribed to and whether his belief was a matter of heart not head are not the subjects of this chapter. What is clear is that the altered status of Christianity as the official religion of the Roman Empire was not universally popular, and Constantine needed ways to unite the empire around its new dogma. High-profile building projects, such as the Church of the Holy Sepulchre, may have been one such way.

The translator: Jerome

Underground, on the same site as the Church of the Nativity in Bethlehem, can be found Jerome's caves, now a pilgrim site in their own right. It was probably through the pilgrimage of others that Jerome first travelled to Palestine. Paula, an educated, well-born Roman woman, who had been part of Jerome's circle in Rome, had determined to spend the final years of her life in the Holy Land and travelled there in AD 385 with her daughter Eustochium, Jerome accompanying them as a kind of spiritual adviser. Jerome journeyed on into Egypt but returned to Palestine and spent the remaining years of his life in this network of caves where, with a few friends (including Paula and Eustochium), he worked on several huge writing projects, most famously translating most of the Bible into Latin, until his death in AD 420.

Whenever I have visited these caves, they have been packed with people and very hot; the idea of spending more than three decades in such a location, reading, translating and writing is challenging to me. Here, so close to the traditional site where the Word became flesh in the birth of Jesus, I salute those whose flesh became word!

The unnamed Frenchman: Pilgrim of Bordeaux

An anonymous pilgrim journal, attributed to the "Pilgrim of Bordeaux", describes travels to the Holy Land which, through the naming of contemporary officials, has been dated to the years AD 333 and 334. The traveller starts in Bordeaux, journeys to the Holy Land through Italy, Asia Minor and Syria, and returns via Macedonia and Rome to Milan where the journal ends. It is thought to be the oldest Christian pilgrimage itinerary, containing detailed travel instructions and distances between stopping places on the outward and return journeys. Whilst in the Holy Land, the writer makes reference to a wide range of biblical stories from both Old and New Testaments, along with some non-biblical legends and practices.

The bishop: Cyril

Cyril, born in Jerusalem in AD 315, became the city's bishop around AD 349. He is a key figure in a number of the major theological debates of that era, not least the Arian controversy, holding views which led him to be exiled three times. Perhaps it was light relief for him to write liturgies for the thousands of Christian pilgrims who came to Jerusalem each year, particularly in the days leading up to Easter, as he is thought to have developed the specific liturgical forms which were used in the city and then spread around the world by the pilgrims as they returned home. It is Cyril who is acknowledged as, effectively, the inventor of what we now call Holy Week, having instigated Palm Sunday processions and daily observances throughout the week, leading to celebrations of the Resurrection on Easter Sunday.

The wealthy Spanish woman: Egeria

A long letter, known as the *Peregrinatio* or *Itinerarium Egeriae* and addressed to a group of women, is another early account of a pilgrimage to the Holy Land. The journey is normally dated to the early 380s, its author identified as Egeria (also known as Etheria or Aetheria) a Spanish woman about whom little else is known for certain. Her ability to travel suggests she came from a wealthy and educated background, while others have suggested that she may have been a nun as her writing is addressed to her "dear sisters". Egeria writes in detail about her journey and the three years she stayed in Jerusalem as well as her visit to Galilee. Whilst in Jerusalem she attended some of the liturgical services founded by Cyril, described above, providing early and significant information about the origins and development of liturgical seasons.

This mention of Galilee is interesting; it indicates that early pilgrims also travelled to the region where Jesus grew up and where he conducted the vast majority of his ministry. Tabgha, a village on the shores of Galilee, has long been associated with Jesus' miracles of feeding, and a small chapel was built there around AD 350 by Joseph of Tiberias, a Jewish convert to Christianity.

Seventh-century challenges

For four centuries from around AD 650, Palestine came under Muslim rule, and the rise of Islam gradually made it more difficult for Christian pilgrims to visit sites in Palestine/Israel. The Venerable Bede makes mention, in his *Ecclesiastical History of the English People*, of Arculf, a French bishop shipwrecked on the shore of Iona apparently on his return from a pilgrimage to the Holy Land. Arculf went on to produce a work (*De Locis Sanctis*, "Concerning sacred places") describing his visits to Jerusalem and Bethlehem around AD 680. This shows that Christian pilgrimage could still take place at the end of the seventh century, but by the end of the eleventh century Christian visits were prohibited. By that date, the Seljuk Empire was holding sway; the expansion and growing control of this Turko-Persian Sunni Muslim empire was one of the reasons for the Crusades, a sad chapter in the history of Christianity which further complicates the pilgrimage story.

Eleventh-century conflict

Recovery of the Holy Land from Islamic rule prompted the Western Church to initiate and involve itself in the series of religious wars known as the Crusades, waged in the eleventh and twelfth centuries. Faithful Christians were urged to respond to the call for what was effectively an armed pilgrimage to Jerusalem. The city was violently taken in July 1099 at the end of the First Crusade (1096–99) with enormous loss of life, and the Crusader "Kingdom of Jerusalem" was established. This unlikely victory, given the relative strength of the two sides, was widely seen throughout Western Europe as the work of God. Since then, perceptions of this period of history have been as varied and as contradictory as it is possible to imagine. Against a background of conflict and confusion, between 1099 and 1291, the Crusaders built or rebuilt many churches in the Holy Land and reopened many Christian pilgrimage sites, such as the beautiful church of St Anne's at the Pool of Bethesda.

In 1219, during the Fifth Crusade, Saint Francis of Assisi visited Syria in an attempt to convert the Muslims. He went directly to the Sultan (Malik al Kamil) seeking to make peace. It seems that an unlikely but sincere friendship grew up between the two men, and the Sultan was so charmed by Francis that he agreed to allow access to many of the holy sites, giving Francis (and Franciscans) custody of them. Many modern pilgrims will have encountered the brown-robed monks at such sites as "Dominus Flevit" in Jerusalem, the Church of the Holy Nativity in Bethlehem and the Church of the Annunciation in Nazareth (and may also have witnessed their custodial zeal).

The rise of European sites

When pilgrimage to the Holy Land was prohibited, or at least dangerous, pilgrim sites began to appear closer to home which were easier to access. Rome was traditionally believed to be the burial site of the apostle Peter and a church has stood on the site now known as St Peter's Basilica since the fourth century AD. The building of the present basilica took place between 1506 and 1626. Others have seen the Colosseum, site of so much early Christian martyrdom, as an appropriate pilgrimage destination.

Two hundred years after Peter's burial site was identified in Rome, it was believed that the tomb of James the apostle had been located in Santiago de Compostela in Northern Spain, and the first church to mark this was built in AD 829. Both these sites attract huge numbers of pilgrims every year, and the network of paths known as the Camino (Way) to Santiago is now perhaps the most famous and most travelled of all Christian pilgrimage routes.

Almost a millennium later, in 1858 in Lourdes, southwestern France, the vision of the Virgin Mary to a local woman, Bernadette Soubirous, led to the establishment of a major pilgrim site there which continues to attract millions of visitors annually. The recreation of pilgrimage sites in more accessible locations, and the development of labyrinths, were additional responses to the increasing challenges of travel—see Chapter 11.

Pilgrim sites and saints in the British Isles

Meanwhile, in the Celtic north of Britain a gallery of outstanding men and women began to change the religious face of the land, and sites associated with their lives became places of pilgrimage. It is in some of these places that I first began to immerse myself in a bigger and wilder God, a God who could still connect with me in my raw grief and bleakness. These are the places where I have breathed in the air of wild beaches, touched the stones of ancient buildings and read the stories of pioneer spirits, finding that all of these saints are fascinating characters worthy of the many books already devoted to them. Such pilgrims are the jewels in the history of these islands, men and women who sought to know Christ and make him known as widely as they could. Some of the sites will be revisited in Chapter 5; here are very brief notes about some of those pioneering pilgrim men and women whose footprints are still to be found in Britain's religious landscape:

- Amongst the earliest of these, and consequently amongst the most obscure, is **Ninian**, first mentioned (by Bede) in the eighth century, but probably a fourth-century native of southern Scotland who travelled to Rome to receive theological training. Ninian is believed to have returned to the Galloway coast, landing on the tiny peninsula now known as the Isle of Whithorn, in AD 397. There he built a monastery, Candida Casa (the White House), from where Christianity began to spread across what is now southern Scotland and parts of Northumbria. Ninian is often described as the Apostle to the Southern Picts.
- **Columba** (Comcille) left Ireland and landed in Iona in AD 563. He built a church, established a monastery and remained there until his death in 597. Since 1938, when George MacLeod founded the Iona Community, building connections between the then squalor of inner-city Glasgow and the wild beauty of this island in the Inner Hebrides, Iona has grown into one of the best known of all pilgrimage sites in the world and as the cradle of much contemporary worship material and social justice activism.
- **Mungo**, or Kentigern, had an inauspicious start to life. His mother, St Enoch (also Tennoch, Thenew or other derivatives) was violently thrown out of court by her father, King Loth, outraged by her unwed pregnant state. Legend tells us that her son was born on the beach at Culross in Fife around AD 525, raised by his mother and the monks at Culross Abbey from where he later travelled to start his own religious community at a "dear, green place" (*Glas-chu*) on the Molendinar Burn and in doing so founded the city of Glasgow, still a city of pilgrimage for the discerning pilgrim.
- **Aidan**, another Irish monk summoned to northern England by King Oswald, won the hearts and souls of ordinary people by

his humble demeanour. In AD 634 he founded a monastery on Lindisfarne, the tiny tidal island off the Northumbrian coast, around the same time as another great northern saint, Cuthbert, was born. Aidan is believed to have died on 31 August 651.

- That same night, **Cuthbert**, a teenage shepherd near to Melrose in the Scottish/English borders, saw a vision of a sacred fire being carried to heaven. Convinced that God was speaking to him through this he made his way to Melrose Abbey where the wise Prior Boisil and Abbot Eata welcomed and nurtured him. Cuthbert and Eata both moved to Ripon for a short time, Eata as abbot, Cuthbert as guest master, until Wilfrid arrived from Rome, via the south of England, and was appointed abbot in Ripon, at which point Cuthbert and Eata both returned to Melrose. Cuthbert and Wilfred are often seen as representatives of two opposing emphases within the church of their day with Cuthbert standing for all that was "Celtic" about Christianity in the British Isles against the incoming tide of "Roman" influence, which Wilfred championed.

- The story is the subject of many books, but not this one. Ultimately it may have been Cuthbert's graciousness which allowed the inevitable changes to take place relatively peaceably. This can lead to bitterness and even grumbling against Cuthbert; his "graciousness" and failure to stand up for his own traditions have affected all our lives. Alternatively, we could step back and reflect that whilst that may be so, in such conflicts, which sadly still affect the church, is it not better to be on the side of grace? Cuthbert became prior of Lindisfarne after the Synod of Whitby (see below) and so began his association with that island for which he is best known. He seems to have been a personable and popular leader who chose to follow what he understood to be the hardest and highest calling, to the life of a hermit, and was a reluctant bishop for the final few years of his life. He died on his island retreat in the Farne Islands in 687.

- Playing a key role in the Celtic v. Roman debate is **Hilda**, a remarkable woman according to all the many accounts of her life. Perhaps the inclusion of a woman as a leading figure in church history and politics in the seventh century makes it inevitable that some of these accounts tend towards fiction and high romance, with others seeking to stick more closely to the limited known facts. Following her conversion, Hilda (or Hild) was known and respected by Aidan and notably became the first person (of any gender) to found a "double" monastery (accommodating both male and female monks) at **Whitby**. So it was that Hilda presided over the watershed Synod of Whitby (664) at which the incoming Roman influence (concerning, amongst other things, the dating of Easter and the style of monks' tonsures) won out over the older Celtic traditions.

- **Bega** is another name associated with the complex and intriguing story of the development of Christian faith in the British Isles. Again, facts are thin on the ground, but it may be that she fled Ireland in around AD 850 to escape marriage, possibly to a Viking prince, and landed at St Bees Head on the Cumbrian coast. There she lived out her calling to purity, probably moving east to Northumbria when Vikings threatened the West Coast. St Bees Head takes its name from Bega and is now the starting point of the coast-to-coast walk developed by the walker and author Alfred Wainwright, which may, by some, be walked as a pilgrimage.

- In the East Anglian village of Walsingham, legend claims, an Anglo-Saxon noblewoman, Richeldis de Faverches, had a vision in 1061 in which the Virgin Mary told her to build a copy of the site in Nazareth where the angel Gabriel had appeared to her. Walsingham quickly became a significant pilgrimage site to which King Henry III made frequent pilgrimages, as did many subsequent monarchs. Such visits may have been seen to lend a "royal seal of approval" to pilgrimage, at least among those of the same religious persuasion. Walsingham remains a lively pilgrim site today, with both Roman Catholic and Anglican shrines, as well as a small Methodist chapel with its own vision to offer hospitality to those on the pilgrim trail.

- Canterbury became a pilgrimage site because of the murder of **Thomas à Becket** in the Cathedral in 1170, immortalized in the drama by T. S. Eliot. After Becket's canonization in 1173, the city's significance as a pilgrim site rivalled that of Walsingham and is today far more widely known. The cathedral is the destination for pilgrim paths from Winchester, Rochester and London and marks the starting point of the Via Francigena route to Rome.

A rough road

Pilgrimage has not always been an esteemed spiritual practice; like so many of the footpaths along which the pilgrim may tread, the road of acceptance for pilgrimage itself has been rugged and challenging. Charges of spiritual or economic elitism, the ever-present dangers of overcommercialization leading to corruption and misconduct, and an association with punishment and purgatory have all served as deterrents to would-be pilgrims.

In medieval times (roughly between AD 500 and 1500), pilgrimage was often used as a penance by priestly direction, or as a punishment for criminals, neither of which might have endeared its practice to its practitioners. One woman of this period, Margery Kempe, seems to have undertaken pilgrimage as a self-imposed discipline. Born in Norfolk c.1373, married at the age of 20 and mother of 14 children with her husband John Kempe, she suffered a serious illness and a period of what she described as madness before experiencing a vision calling her to turn her back on the world. Feeling sexual temptation to be a particular expression of her worldliness, she persuaded her husband to agree to a chaste marriage and set off on numerous pilgrimages to sites that included Rome, Santiago and Jerusalem. *The Book of Margery Kempe* is sometimes regarded as the first autobiography in the English language. It claims to have been dictated by her to two scribes, since she herself was illiterate, and is written in the third person. Referring to herself as "this creature", Kempe describes her life and travels, along with accounts of divine revelation, a meeting with the anchorite Julian of Norwich in 1413, and the continued persecution she experienced from religious and civic leaders on her travels.

During this period, pilgrimage had also become more commercialized and the church or stewards who controlled the pilgrimage sites made rich profits. This led to further denigration of pilgrimage by those who sought to live by purer ideals. Pilgrimage also developed links with purgatory, a doctrine vigorously opposed by the growing Protestant movement. As a young man, in around 1510, Martin Luther travelled to Rome and was shocked by some aspects of the Roman Catholic faith he observed there, not least the corruption and exploitation associated with those arriving on pilgrimage. The Protestant Reformation which followed therefore rejected pilgrimage as both corrupt and unnecessary. The second of these objections can still be found today. Someone will ask me, "Why do you need to travel to find God, who is everywhere?" I can only agree that you don't.

To me this question, and the early Protestant rejection of pilgrimage, risks losing the value of pilgrimage because of a misunderstanding. Pilgrimage should never be an elitist activity, and of all elitisms, perhaps spiritual elitism is the most distasteful. If pilgrims return telling others that they "must go to Jerusalem" (or Iona or Canterbury) with the implication that if they don't they will be lesser Christians, then I can understand a rebellion against such thinking. Place can be important, as we note in Chapter 8, but whilst I would not claim that physical pilgrimage is an imperative, I feel that perhaps Luther went somewhat too far the other way in a tract dating from 1520:

> All pilgrimages should be stopped. There is no good in them; no commandment enjoins them; no obedience attaches to them. Rather do these pilgrimages give countless occasions to commit sin and to despise God's commandments.[6]

We move on, with a wry smile, as we observe that today there are tour companies offering ten-day "Martin Luther pilgrimages" based in Germany in which you can walk in his footsteps!

John Bunyan's landmark novel, *The Pilgrim's Progress from This World, to That Which Is to Come*, published in 1678, did much to redeem the idea

---

[6] From *To the Christian Nobility of the German Nation* (*An den christlichen Adel deutscher Nation*), the first of three tracts written by Martin Luther in 1520.

of pilgrimage for the Protestant, not primarily as a physical journey but as an inner odyssey of the soul. It is an allegory in which the lead character, Christian, leaves behind his wife and family in the city of Destruction to follow the directions of Evangelist through the famous wicket gate and thence to the Slough of Despond and through many other dangers and fears, until he reaches the Celestial City.

Whilst leading a short pilgrimage in the city of Perth in Scotland in 2022 I talked with a fellow pilgrim about this book, which he had recently reread. He confessed to being put off the whole narrative because of that seemingly selfish beginning, that to pursue his own salvation Christian abandons his wife and family. Only a few weeks before this conversation, the lectionary reading had been the passage from Luke 14 which speaks in verse 26 of the need for a follower of Christ to "hate father and mother, wife and children, brothers and sisters, yes, and even life itself" in order to be a disciple. Digging deep for a way of interpreting these harsh words, I had remembered how my father, almost 50 years previously in a church Bible study, had told the story of John Bunyan in connection with this verse. Bunyan, who was imprisoned for a total of 12 years because he refused to stop preaching his non-conformist faith, thereby condemned his wife and children to extreme poverty and dependence on charity. He himself was convinced that loyalty to God had to come before even responsibilities to family: "O I saw in this condition I was a man who was pulling down his house upon the head of his Wife and Children; yet thought I, I must do it, I must do it."[7] Perhaps in some measure, his own experiences provide a better understanding of the seemingly selfish behaviour of his lead character.

The history of pilgrimage cannot be separated from the history of religious sectarianism in Britain and Europe. Even in the twenty-first century, echoes of this still linger, as the next chapter may show. A later challenge to the practice comes from a post-modern culture in which the rise of reason and science demand that all experience be undergirded with authenticity and historicity. Questions such as "Is this really the site?"

---

[7] *Grace Abounding to the Chief of Sinners*, John Bunyan para 328. Free online version: <https://www.gutenberg.org/ebooks/654>, accessed 8 February 2023.

or "How do we know what happened here?" may increase scepticism about pilgrimage. Yet pilgrimage persists and grows, in part through the devotion to it of world religions other than Christianity, where it may be seen much more as a requirement of faith. I hesitate to try to calculate the total number of pilgrimages made in any year, and internet research reveals that most websites hesitate too, but one site suggests that at least 155 million pilgrimages are made every year.[8]

Perhaps history tells us that pilgrimage is part of our DNA, a universal human activity? Perhaps humans have always needed to find bigger and wilder ways to encounter God?

---

[8] Statistics from <http://www.arcworld.org/downloads/ARC%20pilgrimage%20statistics%20155m%2011-12-19.pdf>, accessed 8 February 2023.

4

Methodism and pilgrimage?

"Why would Methodists go on pilgrimage, Jill? What does a Methodist pilgrimage look like?" These questions were posed to me on one of my early group pilgrimages to Lindisfarne. I remember exactly where we were at the time (approaching the delightful village of Low Newton-by-the-Sea), and I remember struggling for an answer. Sarah, who asked the questions, was well qualified to do so; her day job included responsibility for tourism in an Anglican cathedral, and in a voluntary capacity she was chair of the Methodist Heritage committee. Her questions made me realize that I had allowed myself to be swept into this activity by a combination of serendipity, pragmatism and emotion, but hadn't asked all the questions I could have asked. This simple exchange on a sunny Northumbrian day in March 2015 triggered significant thinking, researching and conferring. There were some obvious answers—such as the strong theme of journeying in the language used by Methodists—but there were obvious challenges too—John Wesley does not appear to have used the term "pilgrimage" much if at all; what would he say about what we were doing now?

This chapter seeks to address both reasons and challenges to some extent, but I am always glad to hear from folk who have other understandings and stories to share. Many of the ideas which follow were triggered by conversations held at a short one-off event, grandly called the "Methodist Pilgrimage Reference Group", which met for 24 hours at Cliff College in November 2015. I am grateful to all who shared their thinking at that gathering.[9] A thread which ran throughout the

---

[9] Attendees at the Methodist Pilgrimage Reference group: Joy Adams, Jill Baker, Gillian Kingston, Gill Mackenzie, Tony Moodie, Stephen Skuce, Adam

consultation was the sense that Methodism has something distinctive and important to bring to the journey of pilgrimage, a journey shared with other churches, other faiths, other philosophies.

Language and ethos

Methodism has always understood itself as a movement, in contrast to the more parish-based view of some other denominations. In recent years the strapline, "A discipleship movement shaped for mission" has been widespread in the British Methodist Church and reminded many of their roots as a people on the move, not an established church fettered by buildings and unchangeable traditions. Digging more deeply into the name, "Methodist", which began as a nickname for an orderly and systematic way of discipleship, I was surprised to discover that "Method" picks up a Greek word we have already thought about and couples it with another in a phrase meaning "after the way", *meta odos*, so this sense of being on the move is at our core. Methodism draws frequently on the image known as *The Methodist Quadrilateral* in which the four legs of Scripture, Reason, Experience and Tradition hold up our theology and practice. All four legs can offer support to the practice of pilgrimage, as I hope these chapters might demonstrate.

Newcomers to Methodism soon hear the language of journeying; we group our congregations into "circuits"; the places to which ministers are sent are known as "stations", with all that that implies of onward travel at some point; the length of service of our ministers is known as their "years of travel" (even if they have only served in one station) and when they retire, we call that "sitting down" for it marks the end of a period of "itinerancy".

Stevenson, Simon Topping, Karen Turner. Others contributing in writing: Jane Leach, Sarah Friswell.

Itinerancy

John Wesley himself travelled prodigiously and set up a network of preachers who would also travel—not always as widely as him, but around the new Methodist congregations set up in their locality. Willingness to travel was part and parcel of being one of Mr Wesley's preachers. Itinerancy affects not only those who move and their families, but the congregations too, who may have to say farewell to a minister they would like to keep for longer or put up with one to whom they would have been glad to wave goodbye! Itinerancy has its defenders and its opponents, and this is not a full analysis of the practice by any means, but in the context of pilgrimage, itinerancy can be an outworking of "liminality" (see Chapter 5) which, whilst making us more vulnerable at times, may also make us more open to the Spirit.

Itinerancy has meant different things over the centuries. For the earliest Methodist preachers, it may have brought physical risks and dangers. This makes it all the more remarkable that women were amongst the early preachers of the Primitive Methodist Church, convinced that their faith was a faith to be shared both in the domestic arena and out on the "circuit" as well. As Methodism became more organized, with preachers and then ministers being allocated to particular locations for certain periods, itinerancy developed again. For many years, the standard period of service for an initial invitation to any one place was three years; now (in 2023) it is usually five years, and re-invitations to stay in the same place are much more frequent than they were. This reflects a changing landscape from the days when all ministers were men who, if married, understood that their wives would rarely, if ever, have jobs outside the home, to a much more varied picture. Children and their needs may not have changed a great deal in that time, but consideration of them certainly has. One of the bedrocks of early Methodism, itinerancy is facing challenges in this century, with some feeling it has served its purpose. As one ministerial spouse reflected, "Either it's a prophetic sign of who we are that should be valued (and supported) and a spiritual discipline—or it's a ridiculously outdated impractical system that people go out of their way to try to evade."

As the spouse of a minister myself, I look back and count 13 places which I have called home during Andrew's 30-odd years of travel. Periods of occupation range from a few weeks during training to nine years (so far). Styles of accommodation vary widely too; during our years as mission partners in the Caribbean we spent a few months on a church hall floor while the manse was being repaired, but those were also the years where we were housed in a five-bedroom, four-bathroom manse on three levels, with views of the sunrise from the rear balcony and the sunset from the front! It is not so much the houses, flats, floors and mansions which have impacted my soul, but rather the sense of impermanence. For me, for us, that has always been welcome; the verse from Hebrews (13:14) to which I refer frequently has been a mantra for life, "For here we have no lasting city, but we are looking for the city that is to come", and our experience has been that itinerancy has made life richer and deeper. However, I know that for others that has not always been the case.

Itinerancy has much in common with pilgrimage: moving through a landscape, interacting in worship, shared meals, fellowship and the ups and downs of life with different people at different times, meeting people who have travelled the same road at a different time, travelling lightly, making good endings and good beginnings ... some of this will be considered further in Chapter 9.

Connexionalism and World Methodism

Unique to Methodism (as far as I am aware) is the spelling of "Connexion" with an "x", a quirk which seeks to express that we mean something special and distinct from other ways of being connected (with a "ct"). Connexion is a word which speaks positively of family and relationship, although at times perhaps both of these may feel more like a goldfish-bowl experience where everyone knows everyone else and what everyone else is doing. At the time of writing, Methodism in Britain has something in the region of 150,000 members, so clearly we don't all know each other, but put two Methodists in a room together and the "six degrees of separation" which are supposed to connect all human beings in the world will probably be reduced to two or three. This is largely due to itinerancy, which serves as the underground root system of connection between congregations and individuals around the British Connexion. It is helped along by organizations which have, over the years, brought people together from different parts of these islands to share in worship and fellowship: 3-Generate (and all its predecessor youth movements); Methodist Women in Britain (similarly the current expression of a long chain of activity); societies focusing on art, music, drama, spirituality... when a Methodist signs up to attend such an event it is, I suggest, in the sure knowledge that they will find someone else there whom they know or, at very least, who knows someone they know.

How might this relate to pilgrimage? Those who have walked some of the longer and better-known pilgrim routes, in particular the Camino to Santiago de Compostela, will speak of just such communities arising along the way—travellers you have already met, or ones you have heard about from those you walked with yesterday. Broader than this, all pilgrims are part of the universal "Connexion" which includes all other pilgrims—an idea we will explore more in Chapter 7.

This sense of connection extends beyond the Methodist Church in Britain. The eight years we spent as Mission Partners with the Methodist Church in the Caribbean and Americas (MCCA) in the South Caribbean taught us something of the importance of this global family who know of each other, pray for each other, sometimes meet each other, and definitely feel connected to each other. Whenever I have had the opportunity to visit Methodist churches in other parts of the world, I have sensed very strongly this feeling of all being raised from the same root and of being on the same journey—the journey Wesley envisioned towards scriptural holiness and Christian Perfection (see below).

Wesley's experience of journey

That root is, of course, the faith and discipline of the founder of Methodism, John Wesley. Perhaps the most familiar image of Wesley is that of him on horseback. He is estimated to have travelled around a quarter of a million miles on horseback in his lifetime (1703–91) and could certainly be viewed as a pilgrim. It is unlikely, however, that he would have claimed that title for himself. As we saw in Chapter 3, the practice of pilgrimage has received opposition and denigration at periods in its history and in Wesley's era would have been strongly associated with the Roman Catholic Church. It is possible that Wesley shared Luther's earlier Protestant criticism of pilgrimage as corrupt and elitist and shied away from describing his travels in that way. Indeed, he seems hardly to have used the word "pilgrim" at all. There is just one reference in Wesley's Notes on the New Testament where, commenting on 1 Peter 2:11 he uses a translation (possibly his own) which reads: "Beloved, I beseech you as sojourners and pilgrims, abstain from fleshly desires, which war against the soul." He explains the word "pilgrims" as meaning "those who are in a strange country" and goes on to say, "You are pilgrims in this world." However, there can be no doubt that Wesley valued journey very highly, not simply as a means of getting from one place to the next, but also as a discipline and as a learning experience in its own right. Charles, his younger brother and the author of several thousand hymns, made a happy marriage, had children and settled mainly in one place, whereas John travelled to the end of his life.

The most famous incident in Wesley's life took place in London on 24 May 1738, about which he writes in detail in his journals. Having already attended St Paul's Cathedral for evensong in the afternoon, his journey took him to another London location:

> In the evening I went very unwillingly to a society in Aldersgate Street, where one was reading Luther's 'Preface to the Epistle to the Romans'. About a quarter before nine, while he was describing the change which God works in the heart through faith in Christ, I felt my heart strangely warmed. I felt I did trust in Christ, Christ alone for salvation, and an assurance was given me that he had taken away my sins, even mine, and saved me from the law of sin and death.

All the elements of pilgrimage are there in this brief paragraph—his *departure*, setting out (unwillingly); his *journey*, or route to Aldersgate Street; his *encounter*, feeling his heart strangely warmed; and his consequent *transformation* which is borne out by his words and witness for the remainder of his life. Indeed, the journey Wesley made that day is re-enacted year by year on or around 24 May as a pilgrimage for Methodists and Anglicans together. Only three months after this, Wesley travelled to Herrnhut in Germany to broaden his spiritual experience and so his life on the road, "after the way", began. Methodism was born and other early leaders, such as George Whitefield and Francis Asbury, also became well used to travel. If this sense of movement contrasts with the parish-based ministry of the Anglican Church at that time, Wesley reconciled the approaches with his well-known saying, "The world is my parish."

His journal extracts reveal what might be called a Celtic understanding of life as a journey, an awareness of the spirituality of journey. It was not only the destinations which were important, but what happened along the way. Often the hardships and difficulties are seen as opportunities for God to protect and rescue him; in Scotland on 12 June 1766 he describes a boggy journey from Dumfries aiming for the Solway Firth. Despite the horse being up to its shoulders in mud several times and Wesley being thrown from the saddle, through the direction of "an honest man", Wesley and his companion were able to reach Skilburness, "blessed be God, not hurt at all". He often used travelling time to read and reflect, and gives his advice on how to do it in an entry for 21 March 1770:

> Nearly thirty years ago I was thinking: 'How is it that no horse ever stumbles while I am reading?' (History, poetry, and philosophy I commonly read on horseback, having other employment at other times.) No account can possibly be given but this: because then I throw the reins on his neck. I then set myself to observe; and I aver, that in riding above a hundred thousand miles, I scarcely ever remember any horse (except two, that would fall head over heels anyway) to fall or make a considerable stumble while I rode with a slack rein. To fancy, therefore, that a tight rein prevents stumbling is a capital blunder. I have repeated the trial more frequently than most men in the kingdom can do. A slack rein will prevent stumbling if anything will. But in some horses nothing can.

Also in Scotland, on a May evening in 1763 which was "fair and mild" Wesley preached just outside Aberdeen on the text from Jeremiah 6:16, "Stand at the crossroads, and look, and ask for the ancient paths"—a wonderful pilgrim text!

Another simple definition of pilgrimage which I often use is "learning to walk together". This experience lies behind much of what Wesley says in his sermon on the catholic spirit.[10] Based on a text which is itself from a journey narrative (2 Kings 10:15), Wesley speaks of our relationship with people who have different practices and doctrines in a way which differentiates between "thinking alike" (which may not be our experience) and "walking together" which is the living alongside one another and supporting each other in such a way which we should all be able to achieve. This willingness to journey with those who come from different traditions is one of the strengths of pilgrimage. It is far easier to rub along with another on a side-by-side walk in the open air than it is in a face-to-face meeting around a table in a closed room. "Life lived in this catholic spirit," Wesley concludes, "is a royal path of universal love. Don't be hesitant, press on steadily, firm in the Christian faith and in true catholic love until it swallows you up for ever."

Means of grace

In his teaching on grace, Wesley identified a list of practices which might be seen as "Means of Grace"—ordinary actions by which the Christian might both experience and express more of the grace of God. They include devotional practices such as praying and reading scripture, attending worship and Christian conferring. These all feature in the "Works of piety" while the "Works of mercy" include prison visiting and working for social justice. Neither list includes pilgrimage, but perhaps in a later century Wesley might have considered including the practice. It would certainly fit the bill as a source of inner renewal which can

---

[10] Sermon 34, "The Catholic Spirit" in *Sermons on Several Occasions by the Reverend John Wesley, M.A.* translated into modern English by James D. Holway (London: Morleys Bible and Bookshop Ltd., 1987).

lead to the renewal of the church, and time spent travelling would offer opportunity for reading and praying as well as reflecting on holiness.

Christian conferring is an interesting means of grace and one of which we sometimes lose sight when we attend our many Methodist meetings, be that church council, circuit meeting, district synod, the annual Connexional gathering of the Methodist Conference or the many other meetings which fill our diaries. The idea that meeting and talking together around the challenges and opportunities which face us might itself be a means of grace is, to me, an enriching prospect. Meetings are not just for the purpose of ticking boxes or passing on information but are a fertile ground for the grace of God to be at work within us and between us, bringing about transformation into the likeness of Christ. How might our meetings change if we approached them in that way? Here pilgrimage—in many forms—can play a part. Pilgrimage calls people to walk alongside each other, sharing views, thoughts, inspiration, anxieties, desires; it calls us to listen to each other, sometimes to travel together in silence as we reflect on each other's words and on the voice of the Spirit, and it gives space for us to see issues from a new perspective. It is no coincidence that the Methodist Church's long period of reflection and discernment on sexuality was known as "The pilgrimage of faith".[11] Asked to address this at the Methodist Conference of 2014, I said that perhaps the only rule of pilgrimage is that no one settles for the teashop along the way because it is more comfortable than the journey. I was taken to task by a contributor to the debate who felt that pilgrimage language was inappropriate for such a sensitive issue, as it only works for those who subscribe to the perceived destination. That raises fascinating questions about the role of destination in pilgrimage—see below. If, however, we can at least agree that peace and reconciliation are part of the destination, then we know that to reach them requires the right pathways to be found. As we continue to grapple with contradictory convictions, we could do well to recapture some of Wesley's language of walking together. In some of the physical pilgrimages I have led, the band of pilgrims has included

---

[11] <https://www.methodist.org.uk/about-us/news/latest-news/all-news/the-pilgrimage-of-faith-major-report-on-homosexuality-coming-to-methodist-conference/>, accessed 8 February 2023.

people who really didn't get on together ... but walking in the open air for much of the day can produce remarkable friendships—or at least levels of tolerance.

The scallop shell

The scallop shell has long been a symbol of pilgrimage and has in more recent years become particularly associated with the Camino to Santiago de Compostela, the burial site of St James. The shell links to James' life as a fisherman on the Sea of Galilee, from where, with his brother John, he was called by Jesus to be a disciple (Matthew 4:21). Anyone who has walked the Camino will be familiar with the schematic shell design which indicates the path to take.

Meanwhile, ardent Methodists, and particularly those of a certain age, will be aware of the various occurrences of the same scallop shell in the Methodist story. The little (usually green) *School Hymnbook of the Methodist Church*, published in 1950 and in use for several decades, had such a shell on its cover; slightly younger Methodists may, as children and teenagers, have been a member of the "Shell Clubs" which were held in many churches around the Connexion; many property secretaries will have had communications from the Trustees for Methodist Church Purposes (TMCP) bearing their shield with 12 scallop shells in the design, and the really keen Methodist historians will know that all this is because the shell forms part of a coat of arms associated with the Wesley family. Or does it, and if so, why? Sadly, the full explanation seems to have been lost, as many shells are, in the sands of time. However, a leading Methodist historian kindly did some research for me and concluded that enthusiastic Methodists in the nineteenth century, wanting to provide the Wesley family with a coat of arms, discovered one linked to the name Wesley dating from the fourteenth century which involved a cross and five scallop shells.[12] They adopted it, but later scholarship indicates

---

[12] Martin Wellings (drawing on the section on "Methodist Heraldry", in *Myths of Methodism* by John Vickers).

that no connection can be established between the fourteenth-century Wesleys and the Methodist Wesleys, so it is, at best, a happy mistake!

That leaves us room to speculate, as another Methodist does: "I'm finding it quite funny that the pilgrim shell has been around symbolically in Methodism for all the wrong reasons . . . it's almost as if this clue has been there all along . . . What if what we had to offer ecumenically and missionally was right underneath our noses?"[13] What indeed?

Primitive Methodism

Without having made any kind of study of the possible place of pilgrimage within the Primitive Methodist movement, I noted the following thought in an article written by Jill Barber, published in *The Ranters' Digest* (Issue 24 Spring 2022). The concept chimes with much that I have said about the benefits of walking together. Entitled "Hugh Bourne and the Place of Women and Lay People in the Primitive Methodist Movement", Jill notes that the founder of Primitive Methodism (Hugh Bourne) "advocated 'conversation preaching'. It was how he made his first convert, inviting his cousin Daniel Shubotham to go for a walk, which is still a good way of sharing faith! As Hugh Bourne said, looking back to the early days: 'Our chapels were the coal pit banks, or any other place; and in our conversation way, we preached the Gospel to all, good or bad, rough or smooth.'"

Hymnody

If, as the Preface to the 1937 *Methodist Hymn Book* stated, and it does seem to be widely agreed, "Methodism was born in song", we might expect to find that pilgrimage features in our hymnody—and we will not be disappointed. Although pilgrims or pilgrimage is only directly mentioned in seven hymns in *Singing the Faith*, the current collection of hymns and songs used in most Methodist congregations, the broader

---

[13] Karen Turner.

theme of journeying is found widely. The section of *Singing the Faith* headed "Our journey with God" narrowly misses being the largest section in the book; with 35 hymns (to the 36 under the "Holy Communion" section"). Some of these are contemporary; many come from the Iona Community or other expressions of "Celtic spirituality", while others are long-established favourites. The extracts I have compiled into a mini-pilgrimage below come from a period spanning more than 500 years (further details can be found in Chapter 11).

Looking at pilgrimage under the four-fold pattern I often employ (and mention first in the Introduction to this book) a congregation might be invited to make their **Departure** with words such as "Will you come and follow me" or "Come with me, come wander". If we are unsure about setting off, we may need to hear in "Jesus Christ is waiting" that "Jesus Christ is calling, calling in the streets, 'Who will join my journey? I will guide their feet.'"

The **Journey** might be accompanied by strains of "Guide me, O thou great Jehovah, pilgrim through this barren land" or "O God of Bethel, by whose hand thy people still are fed; who through this earthly pilgrimage hast all our forebears led". We take notice of our pilgrim companions and our relationship with them as we sing, "Brother, sister, let me serve you", acknowledging that we are part of a pilgrim band, travelling the road with others. If, however, there are disputes along the way, we may need to hear "Because the Saviour prayed that we be one" with its hope that by journey's end, "strangers are the pilgrims you intend". "Sing for God's glory" brings to mind the great cloud of witnesses who accompany us as pilgrims; "Sing for God's saints who have travelled faith's journey before us", an essential element of pilgrimage. The beautiful "Earth's Creator" will help us to appreciate the journey and hold in mind the journey's ending (whilst its 11 verses remind us that we are in this for the long haul!). Those challenging sections of the path could be worked through as we answer the question, "Have you heard God's voice; has your heart been stirred? Are you still prepared to follow?" Here too we might fall back on the best antidote to the hobgoblins or foul fiends of life in Bunyan's classic, "Who would true valour see" with its repeated encouragement "to be a pilgrim".

Encounter with God could give voice to any number of hymns, but the dying words of Wesley "Best of all is God is with us" touch on the "grace received and hope reformed" which epitomize such an encounter. Several hymns link such theophanies with our experience as we share in Holy Communion, so "Food to pilgrims given, strength along the way" is welcome and we may move from this holy moment to the charge, "Now let us from this table rise..." to choose again the pilgrim way.

As the pilgrim turns to make the journey home, **Transformed** and knowing that the end of any pilgrimage is the start of the next, words such as "May the road rise up to meet you" will inspire and reassure, or we can accept the challenge of Charles Wesley's hymn for the turn of the year, still widely used at Watchnight or Covenant services, which expresses exactly that understanding: "Come, let us anew our journey pursue, roll round with the year". Indeed, the Covenant Service could be seen as a marker of a year-long pilgrim route which Methodists covenant to undertake year by year.

Although only the last of the hymns quoted above is by Wesley, that shouldn't lead us to the conclusion that pilgrimage (or at least "journey") does not feature in his hymns. Amongst the 35 hymns in the section, "Our journey with God", six are by Wesley and all have iconic status. They include the two Conference "bookends". "And are we yet alive" (*StF* 456) has been sung at the opening of every annual Methodist Conference since 1744; it invites us to review the year past very much as a year of travel, through troubles, conflicts, fightings and fears, constantly sustained by love and redeeming power until we reach Christian perfection (see below). A few days later, when Conference adjourns, it is always with the short gem, "Captain of Israel's host, and guide of all who seek the land above" (*StF* 459). To my mind this is the perfect pilgrimage hymn; I almost always use it to end a group pilgrimage myself and, with its reference to my core verse from Hebrews, it is also on the list of music for my funeral!

Alongside these three annual rites, Covenant and the opening and closing of Conference, the other three Wesleys in this section are worthy of study from a pilgrim perspective:

- "Author of faith, eternal word" (*StF* 457) also picks up on pilgrimage metaphor from the epistle to the Hebrews, speaking of "faith, like its finisher and Lord" (cf. Hebrews 12:2) and, in its final verse, conveys sublimely the ultimate encounter with God, the end of all our journeying: "Faith lends its realizing light, the clouds disperse, the shadows fly; the Invisible appears in sight, and God is seen by mortal eye."

- "Away with our fears!" (*StF* 458), also known as Wesley's Birthday Hymn, is a testimony to personal faith and dedication to God written, it appears, on Charles' birthday and originally published in *Hymns and Sacred Poems* (1749). The seven verses now included (there were at least as many again in the original poem "On his birthday") take us from "earliest days" through the cares, temptations and snares of life to the "heaven of bliss" which is to be part of "the fold" and pledges that the remainder of the earthly journey will be employed in God's praise and proclamation. Shortly after Charles' death, John Wesley transcribed the final verse in his journal on own eighty-fifth birthday, 28 June 1788:

My remnant of days
I spend in his praise,
who died the whole world to redeem;
be they many or few,
my days are his due,
and they all are devoted to him.

- "Come, O thou Traveller unknown" (*StF* 461) would merit a whole chapter to itself and makes a good companion to the notes on Jacob in Chapter 1. It casts the story of Jacob into the language of spiritual journey and is perhaps one of the most remarkable descriptions of its "Sacred Centre", when Jacob wrestles with a stranger at Peniel, with all its tension, ambiguity and mystery. With 12 six-line verses it is (appropriately) not for the faint-hearted and, in my own experience, rarely sung these days, but it remains a treasure which enriches any engagement with it.

Destination/Christian Perfection

As I have already hinted, the question of destination within pilgrimage also contains tension, ambiguity and even mystery. Early Celtic pilgrims were known to embark in little coracles and to go wherever the winds and tides took them; Jesuits in training are still required to undertake a pilgrimage which has no clear route or destination, being guided as they go by the Spirit. I confess that I have not yet found the courage to offer to take others on pilgrimage on this basis—although, interestingly, when I recently mentioned this in a group, several folk immediately said they would sign up for such an adventure. We will return to the question of destination later, but in this context of Methodism and pilgrimage it constrains us to reflect, somewhat briefly, on Christian Perfection. This was the doctrine promulgated by Wesley—sometimes at some cost to his relationships with other theologians and preachers of his day who did not find it convincing—concisely expressed in verse 5 of "And are we yet alive?":

> Then let us make our boast
> of his redeeming power,
> which saves us to the uttermost,
> till we can sin no more.

Wesley's sermon "Christian Perfection" takes as its text Philippians 3:12 (in which Paul does not claim that he has become perfect) and, with reference to many other texts about the Christian's ability to overcome sin, claims that "All Christians, whether new in the faith or mature, are perfect in the sense that they are able to avoid committing sin".[14] Such a state would be the culmination of the work of sanctifying grace, in which we live and move day by day. It may only be short-lived, it may only be attained near death, but Wesley held onto the conviction that it can be attained. Such a hope may certainly be seen as a destination, and all the struggles and successes of life the footprints which may lead us to it.

---

[14] Sermon 35 "Christian Perfection", in *Sermons on Several Occasions*.

Doing pilgrimage in a Methodist way

Before moving on myself to a closer examination of the sacred spaces and thin places which pilgrimage has offered to me, a few thoughts about how we might, in this day and age, share in pilgrimage in a Methodist way.

Wesley's emphasis on "all" suggests that Wesleyan pilgrimage should be inclusive. This is a challenge for physical pilgrimage, and I am aware that I have sometimes been unwilling to make my walking routes shorter, or to subscribe to the kind of service which will carry baggage along the way. Some of my reasons for this will emerge later, but I would admit upfront that I don't think every individual pilgrimage can be fully inclusive. However, I passionately believe that pilgrimage as a spiritual practice can offer something to all. That too will, I hope, become clear in subsequent chapters. The offering of hospitality to pilgrims is something which widens the net of involvement, and Methodists have always been good at hospitality!

Pilgrimage to Wesleyan and other Methodist sites within Britain is (or certainly was before Covid-19) a growing phenomenon. The main four heritage sites—Epworth Old Rectory; Wesley's Chapel, London; The New Room, Bristol; and Englesea Brook Chapel and Museum of Primitive Methodism, Cheshire—all receive large numbers of visitors, some of whom certainly regard themselves as pilgrims, and there are numerous other sites around the British Isles with a significant Methodist heritage. It is probably also true to say that whilst such places are sometimes ignored or taken for granted by British Methodists, thousands of members of the worldwide Methodist family travel annually to what they regard as hallowed ground. There is certainly potential for more work to be done to relate such visits to a pilgrim ethos, encouraging greater focus on the journey as well as the destination.

Pilgrimage which is designed with health in mind would, I feel, bring a light to John Wesley's eyes, as he was committed to healthy living as a means of grace, and I have heard some anecdotal evidence of pilgrim routes in Britain being advised or even prescribed by doctors. Social justice is part of Methodism's DNA and offers more scope for pilgrimage ideas; travelling to Tolpuddle, engaging with marches around climate change, debt or world peace could all employ characteristics of pilgrimage—but I hesitate to suggest that every such walk or march could, or even should, be so regarded. On a few occasions folk signing up to come with me in a group have enquired about being sponsored for some good cause or other, and I have always discouraged this strongly. There are other approaches I know, which could be equally valid in different situations, but in the group experiences I have designed there has been a strong sense of group identity—rather than the promotion of individual causes—held in tension with an aim of individual spiritual development from which fundraising could distract.

The mission statement "Our Calling" which has been in use for over two decades in British Methodism invites us to respond to God through Worship, Learning and Caring, Service, and Evangelism, all of which could find their place in a pilgrimage.[15] The missional aspects are particularly exciting; through walking, talking, mutual support and care, shared food and drink, communal worship, prayer and silence, transformation takes place; emotions come to the surface; inner soul-searching happens and brings about a great realization of self, God and others. Touching the sacred may lead people to confront their own faith or doubt and even negative experiences can teach us about disillusionment, rebuilding vision, in what to put our trust. These can be powerful experiences for someone on the fringes of faith to share in and may prove significantly more attractive than an invitation to a church service.

Finally, a Methodist pilgrimage will almost certainly involve singing. I have paused with groups to sing some of the hymns mentioned above in a variety of outdoor locations; at train stations and bus stops, on the steps

---

[15] Our Calling: The calling of the Methodist Church is to respond to the gospel of God's love in Christ and to live out its discipleship in worship and mission. It does this through: Worship—The Church exists to increase awareness of God's presence and to celebrate God's love. Learning and Caring—The Church exists to help people to grow and learn as Christians, through mutual support and care. Service—The Church exists to be a good neighbour to people in need and to challenge injustice. Evangelism—The Church exists to make more followers of Jesus Christ. <https://www.methodist.org.uk/about-us/the-methodist-church/our-calling/>, accessed 8 February 2023.

of a university college, part-way across the Pilgrim Path to Lindisfarne, around the statue of St Aidan on Lindisfarne and more. These have been transformational moments where being in a group may make possible something from which I would shrink if alone. I have had pilgrims who found this practice challenging and embarrassing and have certainly received the kind of sympathetic (pitying?) looks from passers-by who wonder if we have lost touch with reality, but this is usually accompanied by a smile and, apart from one occasion in a crowded site in Jerusalem where we were, apparently, breaking the rules, I have never been asked to stop! Methodism was born and still offers new life, in song.

PART 2

Day by day as a pilgrim

Why be a pilgrim now?

It's time to move from looking at the footsteps of others, be they saints or scoundrels, and ask questions about our own paths in life. Are we all pilgrims? All the time? Whether we want to be or not? Certainly we are all on a journey from birth to death, a journey which will teach us much about ourselves, about our surroundings, about other people and about God, and I imagine we all want to travel that journey as well as we can. I suggest that some sort of intentionality, some sort of decision or choice to approach this journey of life in a pilgrim spirit can make all the difference to the ordinary day-by-day life most of us live most of the time. So do travel with me through some "Pilgrim graces" and then four possible stages of pilgrimage (there could be many more) and hold them alongside your own life story. My own belief is that pilgrimage has much to offer to each of us, as well as to the wider church and society, if we view our experiences through pilgrim lenses. Pilgrimage is a kind of conversion which affects the whole of life.

5

Pilgrim graces

I suggest that the essence of a pilgrim is not an ability to walk many miles, nor to carry heavy packs, nor to find the time and money to engage in regular treks across counties, countries or continents. Rather the essence of a pilgrim is to be found in aspects of character. Some of these come naturally, others need work—and each person finds challenge in different areas. My hope and belief are that all of us, with the help of God, can develop the inner characteristics of a pilgrim. In a way this chapter is a pilgrim's version of Paul's list of the fruit of the Holy Spirit (Galatians 5:22–26)—these are the pilgrim's gifts of grace, often learned on rough pathways, whether those are physical pathways underfoot or the everyday course of our life. When I lead pilgrimages, I usually have a "word for the day" as a focus for reflection and sometimes for action; when leading a group of women in Rome I selected words which were key in the writing of St Paul: Thankfulness, Hope, Grace, Boldness, Convinced—there is no shortage of possibilities. Most of the thinking about pilgrim graces which follows began life as a word for the day.

Restlessness

The need to embrace Restlessness comes before we set off. It came into my pilgrimage-vocabulary through the quotation from Canon Stephen Shipley given in the Introduction (page 4). I ask myself, and others, before considering the adventure of pilgrimage, whether on the road or from an armchair, "How restless are you?" Is there within us that need and desire for more? More of God, more of life, more of all the things which make up the rest of this chapter? No one can become a pilgrim who is already content with themselves and with their life; there has to be that worm of discontent nibbling away at the edges, or perhaps at the core. I fear that in church we may find ourselves telling children not to be restless but to sit still, and that too much of that kind of behaviour has persisted through into our adult lives. Maybe what we need more than anything is to be restless. So I like to use the word "restless" in a positive sense, to describe a God-given restlessness which compels us to move out of whatever rut into which we have settled and discover a God who is bigger and wilder than we may have realized. Perhaps Augustine was driving at this same thought in his famous prayer where he speaks of our hearts being "restless, until they find their rest in thee". Ultimately, perhaps, rest (in its fullest sense) is not intended for this life at all; could it be that the "Rest" of which the writer of Hebrews talks so much (see especially 3:11–4:11) is held back from us in this life, precisely so that our restlessness and weariness will drive us beyond ourselves to seek our nourishment and energy from God?

Encounter

I am an introvert, so the word Encounter can cause me to tremble, yet I recognize that it is the heart of the good news of Jesus. In the Gospels, we read stories of the disciples turning people away on several occasions: children and their parents (Mark 10:13–16); the hungry crowds who had been listening to his teaching (Luke 9:12); a Canaanite woman (Matthew 15:23). Others, like the blind man in Luke 18:35ff. are ordered by the crowd to stop shouting, stop trying to attract the attention of Jesus, stay anonymous, keep quiet and keep yourself to yourself. I confess I have some sympathy with the disciples; many are the times that I want to turn and run away from crowds and large gatherings, or from conversations which might disturb me. I note that in all the examples above, and in others too, Jesus disregards the constraints of his companions and initiates encounter, and in every encounter there is transformation. The children are blessed; the woman's daughter is healed; the crowds are fed; the blind man receives his sight. What lies behind encounter might be curiosity—not in a downright nosey way, but rather in that openness which wonders and imagines, which asks questions and listens, which is able to walk in another's shoes at least for a few paces.

When gathering a group of pilgrims together to spend five or six days on the road I almost always choose Encounter as the word for the first day. This is the time when we must encounter one another, perhaps meeting for the first time someone with whom we will share not just our days, but our nights as well, as most expeditions have involved sharing twin rooms. People are nervous, and sometimes it's a challenge. I am nervous too—do I really want to overcome my inner desire to keep quiet in order to enter into the lives of these folk? I remind myself again that when Jesus breaks through the barriers which we put up to protect ourselves, when encounter happens, blessing follows. And it does. We share hopes and fears over a cup of tea—perhaps in the Undercroft of Durham Cathedral, if it is to be a pilgrimage to Lindisfarne. People are relieved to discover that others are also anxious; about carrying a pack, about sharing a room with a stranger; especially about the barefoot crossing to Lindisfarne. Encounter releases the realization that other people are, often, quite nice! We wear sticky labels with our names on and commit ourselves to learning each other's names before the stickiness wears off. We commit ourselves to praying for each other, to listening to each other, and I make the suggestion that we should all feel free to ask each other questions as we walk together, but equally we are free to respond, "I'd rather not talk about that." Whilst breaking down barriers, we still need boundaries. By bedtime our feelings of "Why did I sign up for this?" are somewhat ameliorated, even mine.

I will probably also talk about encountering the spirituality of the landscape—the saints who roamed these hills and valleys, the Christian settlements and practices which evolved here, but not much of that will be absorbed on the first night. I will encourage us (me) to take opportunities to encounter other folk along the pilgrim path, for this too is part of what pilgrimage is about. Phil Cousineau in *The Art of Pilgrimage* suggests that being unwilling to engage with others along the way will either lead to the pilgrim getting lost or, more seriously, to missing the depth of experience which could be had and settling for something more like tourism.[16]

Because I have suggested that others do this, I have to force myself to do the same—and again I discover that Jesus was right all along: encounter does lead to blessing. I speak to the guide in Durham Cathedral and tell her why we are here and what we are doing; she in turn tells the member of the clergy who is leading the 3 p.m. prayers at Cuthbert's tomb which is to be our meeting place, and the kindly deacon mentions us during the prayers, giving us a welcome and a blessing. On another occasion, a winter pilgrimage took me, my sister and niece to Durham Cathedral for Evensong on Twelfth Night; the homily was given by the Dean and included the memorable and transformative words, "Twelfth Night is not the ending of Christmas but the enlarging of it"—my heart soared! A little later, we encountered this same renowned clergyman in the Cathedral Close and thanked him for his message. Enquiring about our reason for being there, he enthused about winter pilgrimages to Lindisfarne, "a connoisseur's time to go"; we gladly recalled these warm words over the following cold days! With a group of pilgrims trying out a proposed route in Scotland, I had scheduled breakfast in the café of a supermarket in Stranraer as the shop opened at 7 a.m. At that hour, however, the café had only one young waitress on duty, and the sudden order for 12 breakfasts came close to overwhelming her; instead of becoming impatient, members of the group showed understanding, kindness and sympathy for her task, and she relaxed and took an interest in our exploits, such that we felt it appropriate to give her a card containing a blessing as we left.

At bus stops and train stations, we all tell other passengers and the ticket collector about our pilgrimage and people are interested and friendly. At one of our inns for overnight accommodation, I allow myself to get into conversation with the owner-manager. She has had some tough experiences in her life and holds things together with remarkable courage and energy. In our conversation, she expresses a longing to pack her own bag and join us on the road. Over the four years during which I stayed regularly at that particular hostelry, she never quite managed to do

---

[16] Phil Cousineau, *The Art of Pilgrimage* (San Francisco: HarperCollins Publishers, 1999).

that, but a relationship grew which was certainly a blessing to me. When the fourth group I took to stay there arrived, soaked to the skin after a day of unrelenting rain, she gave everyone a black plastic sack, telling us to put everything in it, even our boots; by morning all was dry and warm.

Finally, of course, because this is a Christian pilgrimage, I remind pilgrims that part of the purpose of it is to encounter God in a new way, perhaps as bigger and wilder than our previous experience. Opening ourselves to encounter is a pilgrim grace which applies to the whole of life.

Attentiveness

Next day the focus may be Attentiveness. Attentiveness to each other, attentiveness to our surroundings, attentiveness to God. "Open our eyes, Lord, to see your glory," we pray as we set off into the day. Let's listen as much as we speak; let's notice those who aren't saying much, those who seem to be falling behind or suffering from blisters or carrying too much weight. In one group, this led to a lengthy pause outside a public toilet (a frequent occurrence with 12 women on the road together) while one pilgrim adjusted everyone else's rucksack straps as she had noticed that not all of us knew how best to spread the weight between our shoulders and our hips.

In Durham Cathedral, someone notices that the foundation stone of the cathedral was laid on the same date as we are meeting, 11 August, albeit 920 years earlier. On the rugged Northumbrian coast, heading north towards Lindisfarne, there is much to draw our attention in our surroundings: sea, sky, plants, people, weather, colour, lonely places, busy places, the way trees grow in windswept locations, the design of walls and farm buildings to provide shelter from the weather ... Walking another coastal path, from St Ninian's Cave in Galloway, the wildflowers in May are spectacular—vast swathes of pale blue scillas, bobbing clumps of sea pinks in shady spots, cowslips and primroses, anemones, tormentil, thyme, vetch ... we enthuse together and share our ignorance or knowledge accordingly. In Bethlehem we observe the stonework around the "little door" into the Church of the Holy Nativity with its signs of two much larger doors which have now been filled in (to stop anyone riding horses in, apparently); we are glad to be reminded that we need to bow our heads to enter this holy place. Attentiveness does not have to be entirely serious; on a path down to the shore of the Sea of Galilee we find information about rock hyraxes which can be seen in many of the trees and are, apparently "quoted four times in the Scriptures" and I amuse myself by composing the Gospel according to rock hyraxes. (Of course, what has been lost in translation is that hyraxes are *mentioned* four times in the Scriptures: Leviticus 11:5; Deuteronomy 14:7; Psalm 104:18 and Proverbs 30:26 if you want to know more!) On the beach at Prestwick, we have stopped to share in midday devotions when suddenly we spot a sea otter making its leisurely way through the dunes towards the sea and we pause to enjoy its pilgrimage.

Cities, too, lend themselves to greater attentiveness; in Glasgow I repeatedly remind pilgrims to "look up". There is so much that is easily missed, including, in St Enoch's Square where our pilgrimage to Whithorn begins, a wonderful stone bas-relief of two women, Prudence and Adventure. Are these not the very two qualities we need to keep in balance in pilgrimage, as in life? In Perth, as we look at a six-pointed star in a high window of the Methodist Church, the minister there, one of the pilgrim band, confesses he has never spotted it before!

In the evening, we gather and share the fruits of our attentiveness. What have we seen and how has it spoken to us? Then we read again the story of Moses at the burning bush in Exodus 3:1–6, noting (as mentioned in Chapter 1) the intentional way in which Moses "turns aside to see" how the bush blazes but is not consumed and that it is when the Lord sees that Moses has seen, that God begins to speak. God does not force us to pay attention—the birth and death of Jesus both take place off the beaten track; it is almost as if God is asking us whether or not we want to notice. What may happen if we do? What may happen if we don't? How many times may I, by my inattentiveness, have denied God the opportunity to speak?

Courage

Whenever I announce at breakfast that our word for the day will be Courage, I see consternation in some faces. What are we going to face which will demand courage? Like Bunyan's Christian, are we going to have to walk between ravening lions, learning to trust that they really are chained? I explain that during the day we will reflect on strength and weakness, on fear and courage and on the journey Jesus took to the cross. How are we feeling now? Setting off was an adventure, but now reality is kicking in—can we face another day? Are our boots rubbing, will it take courage to put them on again, to pick up the pack again—however well the straps are now adjusted—to put effort again into getting somewhere else to rest, as well as building a pilgrim community as we go? Yes, it probably will.

In the same way, it can take courage to keep on giving our energy to our local, declining, ageing congregation; or to keep on bearing the load of caring for a partner, children, parents; or daily to face a job which demands too much ... In an uncertain world, just carrying on takes courage. Within a pilgrim group, individuals draw courage from others. Often on a Thursday evening on Lindisfarne, with the Pilgrim Poles now behind, people testify how nervous they had felt about the barefoot crossing, and it was only being part of a group which had given them the courage to try it. One supernumerary presbyter wrote to me after the pilgrimage saying that this had been her own experience and quoted a verse from William Cowper's hymn "God moves in a mysterious way":

> You fearful saints, fresh courage take;
> the clouds you so much dread
> are big with mercy and shall break
> in blessings on your head.

Courage can take us to places we might never imagine going.

After Peter's death, I discovered a need for courage such as I had never imagined. On the first occasion after our bereavement that I went into a public restaurant with a friend I burst into tears immediately. How could it be that these people were going about normal life, eating and drinking, laughing and being noisy? My friend sat me down, fetched a drink and a pile of paper serviettes from the bar and said, "Courage is not feeling brave, Jill, it is carrying on when you don't feel brave." Wise words, which I have shared with so many people since. Another treasure from the darkness of those days was a prayer in the *Methodist Prayer Handbook* of 2012 written by Naomi Sharp. Andrew copied it out, and we have both used it repeatedly since then. Again, with Naomi's permission, I have shared this prayer with every pilgrim group I have ever led and in every pilgrim talk I have ever given—and I always note people scribbling it down or photographing the screen to capture these remarkable words; thank you Naomi:

> O my Lord, give me the strength today to choose
> generosity over judgement,
> forgiveness over bitterness,
> courage over self-pity,
> grace over resentment,
> so that your honour and glory would be upheld.
> Amen.[17]

Courage (as well as generosity, forgiveness and grace) is not just about us; as the prayer so wisely says, we need to ask God to give us strength. But these qualities are not just about God either; God doesn't force anything upon us. The strength for which we ask is to enable us to choose the path of courage rather than the beckoning, and oh-so-tempting path of self-pity.

In our devotions during the day, we might reflect on the courage of the Old Testament heroine, Esther, who faces the king despite knowing that to do so may be her death sentence (Esther 4:9–17), and we look at Jesus, even Jesus, needing courage as he "set his face" to go towards Jerusalem (Luke 9:51–53). Courage is a decision, not a feeling. In Glasgow, we learn something of the courage of St Enoch as she raised her son, the

---

[17] Prayer from the *Methodist Prayer Handbook 2012–13* "Crossing the Chasm" © Trustees for Methodist Purposes, reproduced with permission of TMCP and of the author.

city's founder, St Mungo. In Jerusalem, we talk about courage on the day we visit Emmaus and consider the resurrection. It is clear that Cleopas and his companion needed courage as they tried to come to terms with Jesus' death, but do we also need courage to encounter resurrection? A young person I knew longed throughout childhood to become a doctor. Bright as she was, she had no difficulty getting into medical school where, to her surprise and shock, she discovered that the only part of studying medicine she enjoyed was pathology. A dead body offered no threat; the worst had already happened and the role of medicine was to find out why. Far scarier was to encounter a live patient needing diagnosis and treatment! The resurrection of Jesus is not a happy ending but a scary beginning and should put us all on our mettle. We no longer have a dead body to worship, analyse and then leave wherever we found it; we have a living Saviour who cannot be expected to stay put, but who will surprise us by bursting through locked doors and locked hearts. It takes courage to follow a risen Jesus. This is a big and wild pilgrimage we are invited to join.

Rhythm

- Breathe in, breathe out, breathe in, breathe out. It's the oldest rhythm of life and (coupled with the beating of our hearts) perhaps the most essential. Keep going—at times you will be very aware of your breath, as I was when asked to climb a hillside from a 3000 m road in Ethiopia to meet a shepherd (a long story, but thank you, All We Can[18] for the experience!). At other times, you take it for granted; the body automatically engages in this most vital of rhythms.
- Left foot, right foot, left foot, right foot. Another ancient rhythm and another building block of pilgrimage. Again, there will be times when you do it without thinking, and times when it costs

---

[18] All We Can is the operating name for the Methodist Relief and Development Fund, an international development and emergency relief organization <https://www.allwecan.org.uk/>, accessed 8 February 2023.

everything we have. How often have I sat in my bedroom at the start of a pilgrimage and wished we were already at the end, soaking up the beauty of Lindisfarne, taking off my boots for the final time, laying down my pack... and realized that the only way to get to that point is left foot, right foot.

Life is all about rhythm; the essential rhythms of our body, the daily rhythm of darkness and light, the seasonal rhythm of summer and winter, growth and dormancy. Rhythm is everywhere; it is the building block of life. However, there can be a shadow side to rhythm as well—for some of us, perhaps for many of us at certain times in our lives, too rigid a rhythm can feel stifling, threatening, life-sapping. We can become slaves of habit, bound to rituals or rules, captured by inertia as we see no way out of a predictable cycle which leads to decay and death. Life seems to consist of nothing but the pointless rhythms of work, sleep and eating; why get out of bed day by day just to go through the same futile circle day in, day out? The desert fathers and mothers, living in the fourth century in isolated communities around Egypt, those wise men and women who seemed to have faced every difficulty of every succeeding century and who still have so much wisdom to share, knew about this listlessness. They called it *acedia*, sometimes understood as "sloth"—not laziness, but an inability to be energized, an overwhelming sense of futility. Such *acedia* is not unlinked to depression; the desert sages saw it as one of the "passions" of the spiritual life, something which comes without invitation but needs hard work to overcome, and they recognized that it may be, at least in part, brought on by investing too much in the rhythm itself, rather than the life to which the rhythm points. Like everything else, rhythm needs balance and poise. Used rightly it can save us from disaster or help us negotiate disaster when it comes.

In 2015, Andrew was given two months paid leave by the generous Thames Valley Circuit. It was, in effect, delayed compassionate leave as Andrew felt he needed some space to take stock after Peter's death before starting a new appointment. We spent eight weeks in a cottage in the far northwest of Scotland (booked long before we knew that stationing would be sending us north of the border later that year) in the region of Assynt, familiar to us from holidays with the boys ten years before. We were there for the months of May and June, although the temperature never exceeded 12°C the entire time! On the longest day, 21 June, we decided to take advantage of the exceptionally long daylight hours so far north and climb one of our favourite mountains, Suilven, setting off much later in the day than we normally would. Suilven is a long way from any road and it takes almost three hours to reach the base (and the same to return) so for us it was at least an eight-hour walk.

Before setting off in bright sunshine at 2 p.m., we spent the morning reading quietly and I opened *Backpacking with the Saints* by theologian and wilderness-trekker C. Belden Lane.[19] In the first chapter, he talks about the joy of allowing the body's natural rhythm of walking to carry us on a journey. Panic comes from the mind, he suggests, and we need to learn to trust the rhythm so that we do not allow panic to disrupt it. The walk from Glencanisp Lodge was a joy with the familiar sugar loaf shape of Suilven set tantalizingly against a blue sky. More joy when we discovered, as we left the main track which continues through the glen, that the John Muir Trust had built a new, wonderfully dry path across the next very boggy stage to the foot of the mountain. We were making good time and in good spirits. The ascent up a steep gully in the mountain's north flank is always thrilling, if challenging. Neither Andrew nor I consider ourselves to be fast walkers and we are accustomed to being overtaken on our climbs, but on this solstice day we kept pace with other climbers, and possibly even gained on a few during the ascent. As we paused to breathe in and survey the views from the *bealach* (shoulder) of this great giant, the weather did what the weather very often does in Scotland; cloud came rolling in from all directions, completely obliterating our view of the foothills, the coast and the way we had come. Above us the summit still beckoned, but we felt as if we were on a tiny island of rock in a sea of impenetrable cloud. To my own surprise, and certainly Andrew's, I began to panic. Continuing our climb to the summit did not faze me, but the thought of having to step off our lofty perch into that insubstantial and blinding cloud definitely did. Not generally prone to panic attacks, I was suddenly on the edge of one. In this debilitating state, the words

---

[19] C. Belden Lane, *Backpacking with the Saints: Wilderness Hiking as Spiritual Practice* (New York: Oxford University Press, 2015), pp. 6–7.

I had read only that morning came back to me: "Panic comes from the mind, but the rhythm of the body is able to overcome the mind, trust the rhythm." Gradually my breathing slowed and I reminded myself that I had descended this mountain half a dozen times before. I knew the path; my body could do this. It was a memorable lesson learned—rhythm is a powerful friend—and one which I have put to use in pilgrim groups when others have needed to face down fears with footsteps. Left foot, right foot, you will get there.

The church has many rhythms, all shaped by the liturgical year with its blend of familiar and fresh, prudence and adventure if you like. Just as we all have our own tastes in music, perhaps we all have to find our own rhythms in this pilgrimage expedition called life, and recognize that what gives life to us may sap energy from others and vice versa. But in the end, I think, the basic truth applies to all, to keep moving, to go deeper, to be a pilgrim, we have to keep putting one foot in front of the other and keep breathing in the Spirit of God and breathing out the grace of Jesus.

Liminality

This was a new word to me when I began reading books about pilgrimage, but it resonated immediately with much that I had already experienced in my explorations. To be honest, I have never used this long word as a "word for the day" with a pilgrim group—they have enough to carry without being burdened down by five additional syllables. Coming from the Latin word for a threshold, *limen*, the word liminality expresses the idea of "living in between" which is a hallmark of pilgrimage. Pilgrims inhabit a space between worlds. If you are a fan of the C. S. Lewis Narnia books you will remember in *The Magician's Nephew* how Polly and Diggory end up in "the wood between the worlds", emerging there from one of many pools and realizing that each pool is the gateway to another world. (Perhaps you also recall how, just before they jump into another world, wise Polly, in a flash of foresight, ties something to the tree beside the pool which will take them back the way they have come. They both shudder at how nearly they didn't think about that, and how that might have precluded them from ever reaching home again.)

Pilgrimage is often described as a "liminal" experience. Being on the road is being in neither one place nor another; it is a transitional experience. The pilgrim leaves what is known to travel towards a destination which will hopefully be welcoming and safe, but the journey itself is a time of transition where anything might happen. To stay for a moment longer with Narnia, this time *The Lion, the Witch and the Wardrobe*; setting off on pilgrimage is like Lucy at the wardrobe door—crossing that threshold will mean her life will never be the same again. It may be exciting, it may also be terrifying; transition is costly, not smooth. Think back on your own life. How did those times of change and readjustment feel? After moving house, after bereavement, after illness or diagnosis, after relationship breakdown ... Sometimes we pretend that our lives are stable, we have reached a plateau, we are in a good place, all is well with the world, and we try to forget that there are no guarantees that the plateau will stay the same. Anything can happen and we can be plunged into shifting sands from one moment to the next. Transition, liminality, are part of pilgrimage and part of life. How can we embrace that?

Noah (Genesis 5–10) gives us a model of liminality. Those days, weeks, months riding the waters of the flood—travelling not simply from one place to another but from one era to another as humanity made a new beginning—were a liminal experience. Sadly, the narrator of Noah's story doesn't give us many insights into the thoughts and reflections of Noah and his company—we can only surmise! The verse I keep coming back to from Hebrews speaks again here: "For we have here no lasting city, but we are looking for the city which is to come" (Hebrews 13:14), so let's not put too much store by how things are now, for they may not stay that way; let's not put our roots too deeply into this soil, for we may be uprooted; let's not build our theology around how things are here and now, for things are very different elsewhere. Itinerancy helps with this as did our eight years of life as Mission Partners in the South Caribbean. The American theological ethicist Richard Niebuhr says something similar, defining pilgrims as "persons in motion passing through territories not their own ...".

Such thinking enables the pilgrim to tread lightly on the ground under their feet, recognizing this feeling of liminality and transition. One path where this always feels particularly appropriate is the Pilgrim Path from mainland Northumbria across to the Holy Island of Lindisfarne; come, walk it with me now. Some of you may have been there, perhaps you have walked it yourself, but if not, kick off the shoes of your mind now and come with me. For this is a liminal experience like no other in my experience, where the physical ambiguity of a walk which is neither on land nor on sea reinforces the sense of crossing between worlds—it can feel vulnerable. It is Thursday, (on the five group pilgrimages to Lindisfarne which I led with Methodist Women in Britain it was always Thursday when we made this crossing; other days are available). I know that folk in the group are a little nervous, for they will be embracing something very different, taking off their shoes and socks and putting themselves at a certain amount of risk. Not too much, for I have carefully studied the tide timetables and am confident that we are arriving within the safe period of low tide and not trying to cross on a rising tide. Nevertheless, the chatter has quietened as we approach the coast, walk first on the tarmac road until we have crossed the current of the river, and then step down from the road onto the mud. Holding onto one another we remove our boots, tuck our socks inside and tie them all to our packs. Most of us in Western cultures are not accustomed to walking barefoot and to the very different sense of connection which that brings to the ground we tread. We are making ourselves more vulnerable as we remove our shoes, but also opening up new channels through which we may experience this bigger, wilder God. Walking barefoot has often played a part in pilgrimage. At Walsingham, for example, pilgrims may hear Mass, make confession and remove their shoes at the Slipper Chapel, one mile from the shrine, and walk the final mile barefoot. Amongst the groups I have led to Lindisfarne, not everyone has been able to go barefoot and that's fine too—but I advise wearing something which can be thrown away afterwards to save a lengthy cleaning job! When I led my sister and niece along this pilgrim route in January 2015, we decided to wear wetsuit bootees, given the likely water temperature of the North Sea in winter. This worked well for the crossing itself, although I missed the sense of connection and felt the rubber to be rather slippery at times; but the efforts it took to remove the obstinate, close-fitting, freezing footwear at the end rendered our hands numb as well as our feet—I'm not sure I would repeat that particular precaution!

We say a prayer; we look out at the island—it's not far, is it? The silk of the sand under our feet is wonderful after the past days of hiking; blisters are blessed by the shallow ripples of water, which is not too cold, yet. We set out towards the first refuge, following the line of poles which marks the safe route. At the refuge, we group together again and check up on each other; everyone is fine, this is not so bad after all. The sun is shining and we feel like proper pilgrims now. I invite the group to walk the next stage in silence—this is a holy moment; embrace it; be open to it; seize it. For me, the silence is as soothing to my mind as the water and slimy mud are to my feet (yes, the sand has changed into mud by now). I appoint someone else to take the lead until the next refuge and I bring up the rear, from where I can check that everyone is still moving, yet still be in the moment. The silence is not silence at all, but it is a break from conversation—we may hear seals singing, we certainly hear gulls crying, perhaps curlews and oystercatchers too. This is a landscape oozing with life, as well as mud. Ah yes, the mud. That's getting thicker now, deeper, darker, stickier and slippier. I have pre-warned everyone that if they feel they need help, they are not to stay silent! Call out; reach out; we are not 12 individuals; we are a pilgrim band, and I see women taking each other by the hand and silently offering support and reassurance, and my eyes are watering.

We reach the second refuge safely—well, someone has fallen and covered their trousers with mud, but no one is injured, not this time (but see *Risk* below). We break the silence as we sing Richard Gillard's well-known pilgrim song, "Brother, sister, let me serve you". Some of the words capture the way in which we have been supporting each other and holding out our hands to one another; there are a few tears in eyes and lumps in throats as we sing.

Whenever I sing this hymn now, I feel again the mud and water around my ankles, the weight of the rucksack on my shoulders, the anticipation of soon arriving at a special destination and the love and solidarity of being part of a pilgrim band.

For the final section, we talk together again, but there is a kind of awe amongst us, the knowledge that we are in a sacred space. The distance between the mainland and Holy Island along the Pilgrim Path is less than three miles but seems to be fluid during the crossing—perhaps that is part of the liminality. With groups I allow 90 minutes, including time to stop and reflect. More than once I have wondered as the crossing begins if I have allowed far too much time—the island looks so close—but an hour later it can appear to be further away!

Andrew and I once crossed in 40 minutes in very exceptional circumstances. It was February, and we were rewalking the route (to make sure I didn't forget any detail before my March pilgrimage). Storm Henry was raging, most strongly in the North East of England. As we approached the shore of the mainland, we convinced each other that it would be foolhardy to cross by the poles and decided that we would walk on the metalled road on this occasion. Yet, somehow, as we crossed the bridge, we both found ourselves climbing down to the sand and removing our boots after all. It was a remarkable experience; blown along by gale force winds (thankfully behind us) we found ourselves running at times with the sense that we could either keep pace with the wind (the Spirit?) or be blown over.

The words from the prayer used annually at the "Festival of Nine Lessons and Carols" on Christmas Eve in King's College, Cambridge often come to mind on this stretch of the journey to Lindisfarne:

> Let us remember before God all those who rejoice with us, but upon another shore and in a greater light, that multitude which no-one can number, whose hope was in the Word made flesh, and with whom in the Lord Jesus we are for ever one.

That sense of crossing from one shore to another being somehow akin to crossing from life to death was never more real than on this windswept February day as we headed for a silvery light which seemed to cling to the shore of Holy Island beyond the grey mudflats around us. The noise of the wind made speech impossible, and we didn't stop to sing or pray! Andrew said later that he had almost expected Peter to be awaiting us when we reached dry land, such was the liminality of the experience.

Linda Cracknell includes the Pilgrim Path to Lindisfarne in her book, *Doubling Back—Ten paths trodden in memory* and captures wonderfully this aspect of liminality:

> It seemed we were entering Cuthbert's domain where polarities evoke his dilemma between solitude and public calling. It's neither quite land, nor quite sea, can be a place of in or out-tide, of seals grounded or swimming, of stalking birds that can wade or fly or float. A place for shellfish that are half-fish, half-flesh; half-stone, half living-thing. The contradictions are separated by only the most fragile veil or transformed from one to the other by a slice of the clock face. It's not difficult to feel you're in a sacred place.[20]

In "Baring our souls", another chapter in the same book, Linda Cracknell gives some insights into barefoot walking as well; describing such a walk with a Kenyan friend, Philo, in her home village, she writes:

> 'When you have your shoes on you're one station removed from being yourself', Philo had said that morning, while we talked about our walking experiences and she recalled her barefoot village walks as a girl. She compared it to separation from the land when we travel by car. 'When you walk barefoot it's like you're talking. There's something that goes on between your body and the earth.'

I wonder if these thoughts have created some sense of what liminality is in your mind? I hope so, but I also remember the session I led on this word at one retreat based on pilgrimage; I sought to explain the word's etymology, to describe liminal experiences and to reflect on how it may be part of all our lives, but after an hour or so, at the end of the session, a man came to me with a question, "You used the word, 'liminality' at the start of this session; can you tell me what it means please?"!

---

[20] Linda Cracknell, *Doubling Back: Ten paths trodden in memory*, available on Amazon.

Risk

Risk has always been part of pilgrimage, with the very real possibility of not returning alive being a significant part of medieval pilgrimage. Whilst things are, hopefully, somewhat safer for travellers in our century, there may well still be physical risk involved in undertaking a pilgrimage, and I have always invited those who come with me to aver that they are responsible for their own safety as far as possible. In Scotland, a member of the pilot group badly sprained her ankle on a rough section of pathway, near the spot where, on another occasion, I ended up flat on my back in a bog. Somehow she bravely kept going until the end of the day, but her injury called forth grace, support and flexibility from the whole group. During a very cold March crossing to Lindisfarne, a small stone became lodged between two toes of one woman's foot. Her feet were so cold and numb that she wasn't aware of this and certainly not of the damage being done until the foot thawed out after the crossing and it transpired that her toe was broken. By the next morning, her foot was too swollen to wear her boots—thankfully the walking element of the pilgrimage was by then complete—thankfully, too she bore this pain with great fortitude and grace. Towards the end of the crossing with a different group I fell into conversation with another pilgrim who, to be honest, had struggled on the route. She, more than any, knew the grace and support of others who held their hands out to her to keep her on her feet as we went. With the shore not far away, she told me how thankful she was to have made this journey; she had attempted it once before, but on that occasion her companion had been taken seriously ill during the crossing and had had to be picked up by helicopter; she had gone with him and so had not completed the walk, which was why she had signed up to this pilgrimage. I think I would have quite liked to know that story beforehand—but maybe not!

However, risk is about much more than physical injury, and it can be an important element in our pilgrim ethos. In church, we are only likely to mention risk in connection with risk assessments and the need to minimize risk, and of course that is all right and proper, but are we missing an element of the gospel by our commitment to avoid risk? Can pilgrimage help us to explore and handle risk? Rosemary Wakelin, in her hymn "One human family God has made" (*StF* 687), asks the question:

> And are we brave enough to join with that great company—
> the cost not less than all we have and are or hope to be...
> As partners of the living Christ, who risk the path he trod,
> with wondering love we find we share the timeless joy of God.
>
> *(From verses 3 and 4)*

Joining a group of unknown people may be a risk—especially for introverts; physically there is challenge and potential risk involved, but is there also a challenge to our spirituality to engage with God in a different way, to open ourselves to the "bigger and wilder" God of my own experience? I think there may be, and I think too that we might all benefit from allowing ourselves to reflect on and engage more with such a risk. The draw of the familiar is something we all experience and at times it is what we need, but we know too that breaking out of any comfort zone will stretch us and will probably enrich us in the long term. When we read the stories of the people of Israel in the wilderness, we see how their long pilgrimage was frequently wearisome and how, at times, the strangeness, the uncertainty and the deprivation made them long for their familiar lives—even if that meant slavery. When (in Exodus 14:11–12) the Israelites say:

> 'Was it because there were no graves in Egypt that you have taken us away to die in the wilderness? What have you done to us, bringing us out of Egypt? Is this not the very thing we told you in Egypt, "Let us alone and let us serve the Egyptians"? For it would have been better for us to serve the Egyptians than to die in the wilderness.'

or (in Exodus 16:3):

> 'If only we had died by the hand of the LORD in the land of Egypt, when we sat by the fleshpots and ate our fill of bread; for you have brought us out into this wilderness to kill this whole assembly with hunger.'

Perhaps what they are really saying is, "In slavery we had regular meals and knew what we had to do all day and how to live; now we have left those safe structures behind—we don't know where we are going; we don't know how to find food and nourishment, and we are very, very frightened." The element of risk had overwhelmed them. We know that same feeling in our churches today and can easily fall into doing "same old, same old" because at least we know what that feels like; to try something new might be to expose ourselves to the risk of failing... though would that really matter?

These stories take on a new depth after visiting the Judean wilderness. Tarmacked roads and air-conditioned coaches may protect the modern pilgrim from the realities of the desert but turn your back on them for a few minutes and survey the wild barrenness around and imagine what it might have been like to live here for 40 years. The idea of spending 40 days here alone, as Jesus did (Luke 4:1–2) is also daunting—it is a place where temptations might well be manifold. The stretch of wilderness to which pilgrim groups are generally taken is on the road from Jericho to Jerusalem, a notorious route in the time of Jesus. Inevitably the story of the Samaritan who helped the beaten-up traveller comes to mind (Luke 10:25–37)—how long might an injured person lie here in burning sun and drought? We might also recall Martin Luther King's powerful sermon which speaks of the need not simply to help the victim but to fix the Jericho Road—an inspirational approach to any form of development work. In a landscape of shifting sands, it is easy to become disorientated—even leaders with a good sense of direction may quail! A clear path may be the difference between life and death, so we understand why Isaiah (40:3) prophesies the coming of a "highway" in the desert, and why Mark echoes this (1:3) and sees John the Baptist as the one who comes to do just that, heralding the arrival of Jesus and creating a pathway of salvation. Entering wilderness, whether physically or emotionally, is not to be undertaken lightly—for the pilgrim in the Holy Land it may be a choice, but for many people across the world, and for many of us in our ordinary lives, it is not a choice, but a circumstance that sends us into the wilderness of grief or of pain or deprivation. Yet it is awesome too and has the potential to be transformational. Throughout scripture the wilderness is a place of learning, and I think that it may contain wells of wisdom which can only be plumbed when one has spent time there. Without (ever) wanting to put a happy gloss onto hard times, to be faithful to my own visits to the Judean wilderness, I have to mention that on each occasion, even amidst the dusty rocks, in a moment of attentiveness I have spotted a tiny plant, perhaps a dianthus, managing to throw up little circles of pale mauve petals here and there. Truly the wilderness can blossom (Isaiah 35:1).

Pilgrimage invites us to risk losing precious preconceived ideas which have been a comfort to us throughout life. Perhaps Bethlehem is the best example of this. As a great lover of Christmas, I was worried about going to Bethlehem. I had been warned that it is not "O little town" and that I should not arrive starry-eyed, expecting a rural idyll. For that reason, perhaps, I steeled myself against disappointment by adopting a blasé, "I'm not going to feel anything in Bethlehem" approach on my first visit. As we queued in the heaving Church of the Nativity to descend to what really is called the "Grotto" and is duly encased in red velour and gold lamé, I was making jokes about Father Christmas. To my great surprise, as we entered that small stone chamber and I saw men and women kneeling in awe and humility, I burst into tears and have loved Bethlehem, with all its kitsch, ever since. But many of the pilgrims I have taken there have had real and long-lasting problems with the town for a variety of reasons: the crowds, the commercialism, the enthusiastic street vendors, the dominance of the Islamic religion or something else entirely. I have had long conversations with weeping pilgrims who wish they hadn't come at all, rather than have their long-held and precious images dashed. Which is better, I wonder, as individuals or as a church, to hold onto our own ideas and hoped-for scenarios, or to confront reality and find that God is still there and still active? To expose ourselves to such disillusionment is certainly a risk.

Peter loved drama and often in worship portrayed stories from the Bible using his own innovative sketches. When, as incoming President of Methodist Women in Britain, I chose "For such a time as this" (Esther 4:14) as my theme, he developed a series of short dramas to retell the story at the MWiB launch roadshows we held around the Connexion. In March 2012, only a few months before his death, he acted out the story in a way which was closer to the edge than previously; many of the 450 or so folk who filled York Central Methodist Church on that Saturday afternoon held their breath as he climbed the outside of the pulpit to make his points. More than ten years later, I still meet people who were there and who have forgotten everything I or any of the other speakers said, but can still see Peter, holding onto the pulpit with one hand (and two feet) as he declaimed his lines. Perhaps for a few moments, such a flamboyant demonstration of a young man grabbing risk by the throat and staring it down made us all feel a little more adventurous. Risk was at the heart of Peter's life and drama; it took him close to the edge, and, tragically, ended up taking him over the edge. Maybe that is closer to the gospel than "Are you sitting comfortably?"

That same roadshow in York in 2012 was also the only one of the series at which Julie Hulme was able to be present. Julie was the last President of Women's Network in the Methodist Church and the first Vice-President of Methodist Women in Britain. During this period of transition, she was diagnosed with an aggressive return of the cancer she had experienced some ten years previously, and so her involvement in the emerging new movement was limited—a loss to all of us. Julie died early in 2014, but we maintained a correspondence for as long as she had the energy, and her reflections on Peter's performance in York that day, and more widely on his life and death, demonstrate her great perception and generosity:

> I was impressed by the way he presented the story of Esther at York, not just his agility, which was enviable, but the way he made it serve his purpose, which was, I think, to unsettle us slightly so that we listened to the story as if for the first time. Not an easy thing to achieve with those who have been steeped in such stories since childhood, but very necessary. And he succeeded, because we were drawn in by his movement, his unpredictability, the risk he was taking, the way he was walking the edge as it were. He took us with him. He made us listen and earned our respect in so doing.
>
> But it was a risk—it's easy to forget that. He could have fallen flat on his face in so many ways. That's what people don't understand about true creativity. The risk of it, the very real possibility of failure and all its implications. The most creative

people take huge, hidden risks. They give it all, lay it all on the line, commit themselves to it body and soul. And they do it knowing that sometimes it isn't going to work and that there will be a big price to pay. The cost of creativity is paid in the private anguish of the artist. I suspect Peter knew that better than most.

Rest

We began this chapter with "Restlessness" and with the suggestion that "Rest" may be withheld from us while we are on the pilgrim path, precisely in order to make us more attentive or courageous, to encourage us into encounter, liminality and risk, so that we find the rhythm of life which will enable us to keep going. So "Rest" may not be a word for the journey, but perhaps we need to reflect on it in connection with the end of the journey, whether that is the arrival at a destination or at death. When I led my first pilot group of pilgrims to Lindisfarne—a brave band indeed—I had chosen words for each of the days, including "Horizons" for the day when we each returned to our homes (see a little more on Horizons in Chapter 9), but I hadn't chosen a word for the following day, when each would wake in their own beds again and which would be a Sunday. As I travelled home myself, I began to muse on the Rest which I was anticipating and decided to send one further word for the day—simply Rest, with no explanatory notes; just do it!

When a year or two later, I chose these pilgrim attitudes in a retreat for chaplains working in Methodist Homes for the Aged, rest again seemed an important idea to include. These chaplains knew well the need to talk about the end of the journey, to blow apart the fallacy that we will all live forever, which sometimes seduces us, to accept that after a long life, rest is the natural and fitting last movement. Whilst I do not anticipate that heaven will be comprised of dull inactivity, I do believe that it will be the place, the stage of life, when our restless hearts and spirits finally find the rest for which they long. The beautiful prayer used at the end of life, sending the dying soul into that rest, is very much a pilgrim prayer:

> Go forth upon your journey, Christian Soul,
> in the name of God the Father
> who created you;
> in the name of Jesus Christ
> who suffered for you;
> in the name of the Holy Spirit
> who strengthens you;
> in communion with the blessed saints,
> with angels and archangels
> and with all the heavenly host.
> May you rest in peace
> and may the City of God
> be your eternal dwelling. Amen.[21]

A group of weary walkers will inevitably spend some time thinking about the rest which awaits them at the end and this may inspire them to keep going. Our lives as Christians, whilst focused on the here and now, are also undertaken in the light of the final rest which will one day be ours; again, we find energy in pondering that promised rest.

---

[21] This is an ancient prayer for the dying. It can be found in the *Methodist Worship Book* on p. 431.

6

Stage 1—Departure

> Thanks be to God for the restlessness which urges action and change; help me, Holy Spirit, to pay attention to your prompting.

Three factors already considered prepare the ground for departure:

- Firstly the likely derivation of the word "pilgrim" (from the Latin *per ager*, one who walks through the land), so there is an element of the stranger, a traveller from elsewhere and a definite feel of motion.
- Secondly the definition given by Richard Niebuhr (quoted in part in Chapter 5):

Pilgrims are persons in motion passing through territories not their own, seeking something we might call completion, or perhaps the word clarity will do as well, a goal to which only the spirit's compass points the way.

- Thirdly, the idea of "restlessness", a sense within—perhaps buried deeply, perhaps shouting loudly—that we are incomplete, that we desire more, that we were made for more than this. We might detect within ourselves a longing for space, for adventure, even for risk. That feeling is a vocation, a call to the pilgrim life.

Assimilating all of the above, we are ready to ask some questions about what setting off as a pilgrim may require from us.

Luggage/Living lightly

What do we need to carry on the journey? A straightforward question which most of us consider most days, whether it's remembering what we need for a particular meeting or event, or an overnight stay, or from the shops, or even what needs to be fetched from upstairs. Carry too little and you may be unprepared for life; carry too much and you will be weighed down. From Noah onwards, the question of what to take on the journey has been critical. Pause and reflect for a moment—do you have a sense of being burdened down on the journey of life? Of course there are responsibilities which we have to carry, different for us all, but are we also refusing to put down stuff—possessions, emotions, anxieties—which needs to be discarded?

In 2017, Andrew and I travelled to Jerusalem without a group as part of his sabbatical. We flew from Glasgow to Heathrow to Tel Aviv, but our luggage remained in Heathrow. We arrived in a very hot Jerusalem without sun cream, toothbrushes, nightclothes or even a change of clothes (having decided to keep our hand luggage to a minimum, a practice which we have not repeated). It was awkward and expensive, but it was also quite liberating to have so little. When our cases caught up with us 48 hours later, we wondered why on earth we had packed so much stuff!

Prioritizing what we need for any journey, including the journey of life, is essential, but tricky. What is your method when packing for a holiday? Find the bag you want to take, fill it, then stop? Or pile everything you would like with you onto the bed and then find a bag (or bags) which will hold it all? Baggage is critical for a pilgrim and for walking pilgrimages I issue a packing list, which has become shorter over the years. With my initial pilot group, I was a little surprised at the end of the first day to discover that five of the eight women had brought hairdryers with them, something I would consider an unnecessary burden (not to mention futile vanity on the windswept coast of North East England!), but we all have different priorities and it is more important that a pilgrim learns not to judge others who take a different approach. Probably the question I have been asked most frequently by "my" pilgrims is why we don't employ a luggage service to carry our bags from one resting place to the next. Perhaps as I get older this will feel like a more attractive prospect, but my answer at present is twofold. Firstly, if you have carried a rucksack on your back for a number of days, containing everything you need for the journey which can't be found along the way, nothing can compare with the feeling of not having to shoulder that pack again when you finally reach your destination. Secondly, and more importantly, carrying a pack forces us to make choices to leave certain things behind, an essential part of the pilgrim ethos. I have sometimes joked that if we used a luggage carrier people might be tempted to bring tumble dryers as well as hairdryers. Learning to live lightly is an invaluable art. Whether walking home from the shops or climbing a mountain, we all know that carrying too much weight causes pain and slows down the journey; it may even mean that we give up. It affects not only the shoulders, but the knees and the feet—heavy packs cause blisters.

It will also affect the rest of the pilgrims with you. In one group, one of the pilgrims was unaccustomed to walking much at all and didn't really enjoy it but had challenged herself to make the pilgrimage for just that reason. Very soon her feet were blistered and sore, making each step painful. She bore this with great courage and hardly complained, but her roommate noticed the condition of her feet at night and suggested that we should all carry something from her pack to lighten her load. At first, she was very resistant to this idea, but was eventually convinced that the whole group would benefit from being able to walk at a slightly faster pace than she could manage and so, in the middle of a field, her belongings were shared out and the pilgrim band as a whole had a new spring in our step. We often sing of the need for grace to let others serve us and now it was time to live that out.

As we reflect on our lives, are there weights we are carrying which are affecting not just our own journey, but that of our family or congregation? Carrying long-held grudges is hard work; jealousy and discontent weigh heavily; nostalgia can become a dead weight in the heart and mind; unforgiveness rubs savagely at tender skin. It takes courage to travel lightly, to leave favourite books or clothes behind, and it takes courage to lay down weighty emotions and refuse to pick them up again "just in case". How can the Church, at local or national level, discern what to keep from the past and what to throw out of the backpack because it is making our journey painful or slow? Only when we travel without something for a while can we be freed from its unconscious tyranny—whether a hairdryer or a heresy, too many clothes or too many rituals.

Of course there are some essential items a pilgrim must carry, some of which we looked at in Chapter 5. The Baptist theologian and preacher C. H. Spurgeon writes this in his commentary on Psalm 84: "A company of pilgrims who have left their hearts at home will be not better than a caravan of carcasses."[22] Perhaps the question we ask needs to be, "What can we not do without?" The years of the Covid-19 pandemic have thrown up some surprising answers to that question. Do we need to do things in the way we have always done? Do we need buildings? For me, part of discovering God to be bigger and wilder was very much intertwined with being outside. I do believe that God has an affinity with the wild, the unrestricted and the free; sometimes that's easier to find walking on a Northumbrian coast in a gale than it is in church. A book I have already referred to, *Backpacking with the Saints* by C. Belden Lane, suggests that much of the narrative of the Bible takes place outdoors and yet we almost always only read it inside, in our homes or in church. In Britain, we are often at the mercy of the weather but, when possible, it has been a wonderful experience on pilgrimages to read Bible passages in the open air and, often, to "get it" in a new way. I recommend Psalm 104 for this, and most of the Gospels too.

Separation

Linked to the idea of living lightly, but a slightly different perspective on it, is the need to come to terms with separation in our lives. Many of us struggle with it, from small children at the school gate to grieving families and friends at a funeral. We sense the threat of separation at many points in our lives, and usually resist being parted from places, people, occupations or habits which have become familiar and comforting. Perhaps this is part of the human condition with which the writers of the early chapters of Genesis were trying to grapple. Whatever else the remarkable story

---

[22] *The Treasury of David*, Charles H. Spurgeon <https://archive.spurgeon.org/treasury/ps084.php>, accessed 15 February 2023.

of Adam and Eve in the Garden of Eden might mean and point towards, it certainly brings about separation as the couple are expelled from the garden and from their harmonious relationship with fruit-bearing, be that through tilling the earth or through childbearing. One of the most vital, and hardest, lessons of life is to learn to say goodbye well.

On the first evening of any group pilgrimage, I will invite pilgrims to think about the people they have left behind to come on this adventure, whatever emotions that may arouse. Christians do the same year by year at All Saints Tide as we give thanks for those who showed us something of God's light, but who we see no longer. We mark anniversaries, of births and of deaths, of marriages and of divorces, of pregnancy loss and of unrealized hopes, all in an attempt to deal with the reality of separation. I spoke to a woman once who had set up an old church as an art studio with various exhibitions and installations during the year. Whatever the theme of the current exhibition, she told me, people turn it into a memorial—they want to write the names of loved ones who have died on stones, on leaves, on fabric, on paper . . . whatever we suggest, it ends up being a monument to separation. If the pilgrim can be more aware of separation and recognize it as a companion along the path of life, it may lead to the ability, despite the pain, to remember with thankfulness what has been lost rather than to be destroyed by its absence.

The Bible is full of people setting off on journeys, sometimes with enthusiasm and faith, sometimes kicking and screaming, sometimes inscrutable regarding their own emotions. Abram/Abraham is a notable example, especially given that he was not in the first flush of youth. In Genesis 12, he hears and obeys God's call to set out to a land which God will show him. That's all. That, in my reckoning, is extreme pilgrimage. In the New Testament, Luke particularly seems to see life as a journey and tells the story of Jesus' pilgrimage from manger to tomb with both poetry and passion. We have many anecdotes and stories for which to thank Luke, and one to which I frequently return is the description of the women who accompanied Jesus (Luke 8:1–3). He gives us names; he gives us some biographical detail so we know that these women included some who had been demon-possessed and at least one with a high-ranking husband. All these women, travelling with Jesus and the disciples, "provided for them out of their resources". Turning that word around just a little we can view these women as resourceful women, and I reckon they would have needed to be. How risky was it for them to travel with Jesus in first-century Palestine? Did they risk reputation, domesticity, family? What made them set off? I like to see this band as an early pilgrim band, and I want to journey with them, not to be static but always travelling on with Jesus.

In Chapter 1 we looked at the pilgrim story of Rebekah, and her courageous departure from home. Rebekah makes me reflect on my own life; when I have been asked, "Will you go?", how did I respond? What about you? These days I look at my younger self with some surprise—I don't have the same level of nerve I once had and find my anxiety level increases when I undertake adventure. I'm not saying it's easy to become a pilgrim. Before co-leading a Methodist Women in Britain group to Palestine/Israel in November 2015, I was extremely anxious. The day before I was due to fly from Glasgow to Heathrow to meet the rest of the group, I was leading worship with my own little congregation at Anniesland Methodist Church. I based the service around pilgrimage and asked the congregation what they were carrying which needed to be laid down. Leaving a pause for reflection I looked at the wall at the back of the church and could almost see the hand of God writing the word "anxiety" before my eyes. I knew that I had to lay down this near-debilitating level of anxiety and in the coming days God did meet me in that pilgrimage. But I am slow on the uptake and have to relearn that lesson almost every time.

For me the invitation to embark on physical pilgrimage lies in a paradoxical text in Matthew 28. When the women (some of them the same as those Luke has told us about) go to the tomb on the first Easter morning, they meet an angel:

> But the angel said to the women, 'Do not be afraid; I know that you are looking for Jesus who was crucified. He is not here; for he has been raised, as he said. Come, see the place where he lay' (verse 6).

Here is the paradox: "He is not here", but "Come, see the place where he lay." On my first visit to Jerusalem I went, as all pilgrims do, to the

Church of the Holy Sepulchre—and didn't really like it. The crowds were overwhelming and the queue to enter the sepulchre itself was long. Our guide on that occasion advised returning in the early hours of Sunday and this appealed to us, thinking again of those women who, while it was still dark, went to the tomb. So Andrew and I returned at 6 a.m. on Sunday when the queue was much shorter. We waited our turn and entered, along with the man just in front of us, who was carrying under his arm a very large statue of Mary. So there we were, a stranger, the Virgin Mary, Andrew and I, all kneeling beside this stone catafalque. I wondered what I was supposed to feel or do. I looked up and saw a small sign, in Greek, *Christos aneste*, Christ is Risen, and I almost laughed out loud. All this money, all this travelling, all this planning, and now he's not even here! It led me to a rich vein of contemplation in the following months about the presence and absence of God, a line of thought which is a useful companion to any pilgrim. As R. S. Thomas says in his poem, "Pilgrimages":

> ... He is such a fast God,
> always before us and
> leaving as we arrive.[23]

So we respond to the invitation to become a pilgrim knowing that there is no guarantee that God will play by our rules. Although it caused me to tremble, I appreciated and recognized myself in an anecdote told by Phil Cousineau in *The Art of Pilgrimage*; he recounts meeting a woman who had organized a pilgrimage with close attention to detail. Expecting, perhaps that he would commend her, she must have been more than a little disarmed when he expressed the hope that not everything would go to plan, advising her to leave room for serendipity so that the divine might enter in.

---

[23] R. S. Thomas, "Pilgrimages", in *Collected Poems 1945–1990* (London: Dent, 1993), p. 364. Reproduced with permission of Orion Books through PLSclear (78860).

7

Stage 2—The Pilgrim Path

Thanks be to God for the pilgrim path which lies ahead;
help me, Jesus Christ, to walk in step with you.

With the decision to travel made and the packing done, the journey, the pilgrim path, lies ahead. This is where most of the time on pilgrimage is spent, and this is our main teacher. We learn from the path. The spirituality of the journey is discovered in what we learn along the way about ourselves, about the world, about other people, about God. What are the pilgrim paths you are treading at this time? Health? Family? Relationships? Ageing? Discovering God? Employment, unemployment or retirement? Involvement in church? What are these roads teaching us, how attentive are we being to the pilgrimage of life? Any journey needs intentionality: it is a daily, hourly, step-by-step choice to keep going. Sometimes that's relatively easy, sometimes it's hugely demanding. What are the factors we need to consider as we step out? Three questions might be: Which way do we go? Is anyone else on the journey? How long will this take?

Which way do we go?—Direction

Now the pilgrim needs to decide which direction to follow. For me, this opens up the very real possibility of getting lost for I have a poor sense of direction. Indeed, it is worse than that, I have a strong sense of direction, but it is very often wrong. I have been lost or confused in many places, including a memorable day when it took me 25 minutes to find the direction I wanted out of Leeds railway station. The first time I set out on my own to lead a group of pilgrims up the east coast of England from Alnmouth to Lindisfarne my husband offered me a blessing before I left home: "May the sea be always on your right."

Direction may be determined by different considerations—for the groups I have taken there has always been a clear destination in mind and therefore a very real potential for going in the wrong direction. I recognize that this does not give free rein to the style of pilgrimage which is not tied to a route, but instead allows the wind of the Spirit to blow where it will. Maybe in the pilgrimage of life we need to take something from both approaches.

Sometimes when I am lost (and I am thankful to say this usually only happens when I am on my own, as before I take others anywhere I do full reconnaissance) I invoke the wisdom which was not available to earlier pilgrims, some form of satellite navigation. This is not always immediately helpful to me as it might instruct me to head north, and I haven't packed my compass in my handbag today. However, if I set off south, west or east by mistake, I will soon know about it because the estimated time of arrival will get later rather than earlier. I have been known to attempt three different roads at a crossroads before I find the one which reduces the journey time. This too could be a lesson for life; do we sometimes need to set off in the wrong direction for a while rather than standing still, which won't get us anywhere? Can churches take the risk of failing, rather than stagnating as we worry about what to do next?

In Matthew 2, we have the surprising story of the magi who came to Bethlehem to visit the infant Jesus. I say surprising, because really these were the kind of folk who shouldn't be in our nativity sets or on our Christmas cards. Exactly who or what they were is difficult to ascertain, but we do know that reading the future in the stars, divination, was outlawed by Hebrew law (Deuteronomy 18:10); that their name links them to the practice of magic and that sorcerers and those casting spells are similarly outlawed in the same and subsequent verses (although it must be noted that there is more than a little ambiguity about some of these practices, their use, abuse and prohibition). Certainly they were not Jews. Is that why Matthew tells us that they didn't find the right path straightaway? Is there a subliminal message here which allows for pagans and foreigners to encounter the living God, but notes that they may miss the path on occasion? Perhaps; or is this the fanciful imagining of someone trying to see every journey as a moral tale? Certainly they get it wrong in a spectacularly awful way which leads to widespread heartbreak and violence when the jealous King Herod goes on to order the death of all children in and around Bethlehem aged two or less. They choose to return home by a different route—do we understand that to be because they are now different people? But let's leave the subject of transformation to Chapter 9. Other travellers to Bethlehem, described by Luke in the first two chapters of his Gospel, experience many of the emotions of pilgrimage; I reflect on the courage of and risk for Mary, the attentiveness of Joseph, the encounter of the shepherds with the angels and the liminality of that night for all concerned—the unwitting transition from BC to AD. Later in Luke 2, we have the charming story of Jesus getting lost on the way back to Nazareth, or, rather, of his parents losing him. It's interesting that in Luke's Gospel narrative, after this return to Nazareth with his parents, Jesus doesn't go to Jerusalem again until he "set his face" to go there (9:51) for the drama of his final weeks. This is the determination and resolve often needed to set foot upon a particular stretch of the pilgrim path of life.

A final thought on direction might come from Acts 16:6–10 where Paul and Luke are discerning the way forward during Paul's second missionary journey. We hear that they have been "forbidden by the Holy Spirit" to go in one direction, and then after attempting another, find that the "Spirit of Jesus did not allow them". So they head elsewhere until Paul receives the vision inviting them to "Come over to Macedonia and help us", and they become convinced that must be the way to go. In all our planning and wondering about the course of our lives, it is openness to the Spirit of God which lies at the heart.

Is anyone else on the journey?—Community

A vital aspect of the pilgrim path of life is the company we keep as we travel, and this has been (mainly) a source of great joy in the groups I have led. One of the basic tenets of pilgrimage is that you are not alone; even if you choose to walk alone, as many do, you cannot avoid being part of the pilgrim band which has walked that way before you and will do so after you. In Christian life, we call this the company of saints, or the great cloud of witnesses. Throughout the Christian era the importance of that pilgrim band has been recognized. Again, the letter to the Hebrews expresses it beautifully:

> Therefore, since we are surrounded by so great a cloud of witnesses, let us also lay aside every weight and the sin that clings so closely, and let us run with perseverance the race that is set before us, looking to Jesus the pioneer and perfecter of our faith, who for the sake of the joy that was set before him endured the cross, disregarding its shame, and has taken his seat at the right hand of the throne of God. (Hebrews 12:1–2)

From those who have gone before we draw strength for the journey and determination to make it. If they did so, with all the hardships they experienced, it's not on my watch that the baton will be dropped. When life or ministry are tough, this might be the driving force that keeps us on the road, maybe the only one. There's no shame in that; it's part of the pilgrim's experience. There may be higher motivating forces to draw on, but when they elude us, we go with what we can find to give us strength for the journey.

As individuals we may bring particular company with us from amongst those whom we have loved but see no longer and we begin with these companions, before moving on to those who are still alive and physically with us. Whether we see those who have died as spurring us on or nagging us not to give up, they are an important part of the pilgrim band and there is a sense in which we carry them with us, as we do in life. A story from the life—or rather the death—of Saint Cuthbert speaks to me in this context. Cuthbert died on the island of Inner Farne, and his original burial place was Lindisfarne, where miracles were soon claimed by those visiting his grave. This set Cuthbert on the path to sainthood. In 698, eleven years after his death, the monks disinterred his remains so that the bones could become relics and the sainthood be declared. To their surprise Cuthbert's body was undecayed which somewhat raised the game and created a major cult around both Cuthbert and Lindisfarne.

Almost a century later, Viking raids began which wreaked havoc in much of the northeast of England, and certainly in Lindisfarne, for decades. The survivors of the battered community decided to leave the island, probably in 875, with faithful monks carrying Cuthbert's coffin. The community settled for a long time (over a century) in Chester-le-Street but moved again following fears of further attack, finally settling in Durham, where in 1104 the cathedral was dedicated as a fitting monument to Cuthbert. In St Mary's Church on the island of Lindisfarne is a remarkable carving, "The Journey" by local artist Fenwick Lawson which depicts this faithful journey by a group of monks, who carried their dead brother over many miles and many years.

Often on the evening before the crossing to Lindisfarne I have related this story to a pilgrim group, giving them another perspective to the walk they would undertake the next day. One such group included a presbyter whose colleague had recently died suddenly, leaving her with additional responsibilities on top of her own personal loss. I think it was as much of a surprise to her as it was to the monks discovering Cuthbert's uncorrupted remains that, next day, she wept uncontrollably for the entire crossing, feeling that, like those bygone monks, she had been carrying the body of a saint for a long time and finally had the big, wild space she needed to allow her emotions to surface.

The story, and this experience, have led me to reflect a little on the sacrament of carrying a dead body. It is not something which all of us experience; some will have been pall bearers at a funeral and known something of the physical weight of that role, as well as the emotional weight. After the funeral of Her Majesty Queen Elizabeth II, many people noticed and commented on the ministry of those who bore the coffin along its journey. Many women will have, at some time in their life, carried in their womb a foetus whose heart has stopped beating; some will not have been aware of this experience, others will have been acutely sentient to what is happening, and may have carried the weight of heartbreak as well. War often gives us heroic stories of those who have carried the dead body of a friend or brother back from the front line to provide a decent burial. Such experiences are not stages which any of us would choose in the pilgrimage of life, but perhaps there is a sense of the sacred in such devotion and such grief. The carving "The Journey" never fails to move me, especially since a friend pointed out that the hands of the monks are not touching the coffin—they are raised ready in case they need to prevent it from falling at any point, but there is a sense of respect for the saint's remains which speaks to me of the holiness of death and even of the privilege of being one who, however reluctantly, carries to its final resting place the body of someone who has died.

The companions who we can see and hear along the way give us a different kind of encouragement—or we hope they do. We all know how the comments of others can renew our energy or sap it, and so the call to be a pilgrim is a call to find ways of encouraging others on the way, not disheartening them. Sometimes in a pilgrim group there is a personality clash—it is real life after all. The group becomes a microcosm of human relating and everyone is needed to play their part in sorting things out. That doesn't mean everyone in the group needs to have their say, far from it, but some will pray quietly, and some will find techniques of distraction, while one or two trusted folk ask the questions which need to be asked to bring difficulties into the open. It has to be done when a group is on the road together for there is nowhere to hide. Sometimes in the wider experience of life it may be possible—and beneficial—to put distance between those who can't agree at least for a period of time. I am reminded of Paul and Barnabas having a "sharp dissension" in Acts 15 and therefore separating, but I wonder whether the close companionship of pilgrims making a physical journey together and needing to find ways to rub along is not a better image of heaven.

I began this section by saying that we never walk the pilgrim path of life alone—there are always others who have gone this way before and those who will follow and, somehow, we are connected to them. Whilst this remains true, it is also the case that in life many of us find ourselves, at times, alone and perhaps lonely. This may be through bereavement or separation, the ending of a long partnership. Sometimes such endings are peaceful, but often they are accompanied by grief, bitterness, recrimination, regret, even the dreaded self-pity. Does the pilgrim way of life have anything for such times? Without having experienced this sort of aloneness I feel ill equipped to comment, other than to note that with the recent groups I have taken on pilgrimage I have included in each day's walking a short time of silence, perhaps half an hour at the most. It is interesting to note how people respond—some love it. Gone, for a short period, is the need to engage with others, leaving the mind free to engage with the self, with the environment, with God, or perhaps with nothing at all. Others find it challenging—some seem incapable of remaining quiet, although I try to impress upon everyone that this only works if we all stick to it! Perhaps the same is true in life, that periods on our own, which may not be a personal choice but are foisted upon us by circumstance or someone else's decision, work differently for us all. I believe that there is great value in learning to walk alone, and that the times when we do so are potentially times of great personal growth, but what would I know?

How long will this take?—Timing and pace

Any pilgrim journey—whether physical or not—needs to include space for prayer and reflection. In group pilgrimages, we will have regular times of worship morning and evening, perhaps midday too, and be open to the possibility of additional pauses en route—this is not a route-march. I have written already of the holiness of times of prayer and singing during the pilgrim crossing to Lindisfarne, but any location can lend itself to this prayerful attentiveness. The route I have used a few times in Scotland passes alongside the eleventh-century Glenluce Abbey. Historically associated with light (hence Glenluce, from the Latin *lux*), it has long been connected with prayers for healing, especially of blindness or other conditions of the eye. So we will always find time to pause in the abbey grounds and share together the names of those for whom we pray.

I have said already how crucial timing is on the day of the crossing to Lindisfarne. It was Geoffrey Chaucer, author of that classic pilgrim text *The Canterbury Tales*, who first wrote that "Tide and time wait for no man". (It applies to all genders.) So, before a Lindisfarne pilgrimage is even advertised, I need to consult the tide timetables and make decisions about the journey. If the safe crossing time falls early in the day, we may have to miss out one stage of the walk, catch an extra bus and be sure we are at the causeway at the right time. But even catching a bus brings with it anxiety—especially if (as on one occasion) I have not taken into account the difference between summer and winter timetables and have planned to catch a bus which no longer goes where I hoped it would! That particular group of pilgrims were very patient with my mistakes, and thankfully it was a day when we had helpful tide times and were in no danger.

All this makes me ask myself about the part timing plays in my life and about how I respond when things don't happen when I would like them to happen. In his letter to the Galatians, Paul talks of the incarnation of Jesus as happening "When the fulness of time had come" (Galatians 4:4). In my teenage years, I recall being repeatedly told that God's timing is perfect and that if my prayers weren't being answered it was because I needed to wait. Much of that is true, but this needs to be balanced out with those references in scripture to the urgency of the mission. There are some things about which we should be impatient; there are some windows of opportunity for the Church which will not be open for much longer (indeed, many have already closed); there are some crossings which have to be made now, before the tide comes in.

Patience is a virtue, but so, at times, is impatience. Jesus did not always allow people to have as long as they liked to think about something—his answers to two would-be pilgrims in Matthew 8 (18–22) seem terse, but they bear this out. The pilgrim path provides many opportunities to reflect on timing and on pace. As the leader, I have a responsibility to keep the group moving and together. But fitness levels will vary, as will mindsets. It is often said that a group needs to go at the pace of the slowest, but I would temper that a little. The pacing of the day is crucial for a group with a destination to reach—although there may be nine hours available on a particular day between finishing breakfast in one location and sitting down to dinner in another, and only nine miles to cover that day, it would not be a good idea to walk at one mile per hour. The destination needs to be reached before the effort of the journey becomes too much, before apathy or discouragement sets in, before the excitement has worn off. I have seen this not only in leading walking pilgrimages, but also as a tutor for local preachers in the Methodist Church. There may be five years available to complete the course, but to spread it out over five years would be disastrous for some students. The journey has to become the main thing, its own motivation, so that the destination will be reached with enough energy left to enjoy being there. Some of the journeys we have made as a denomination in recent years have needed to pay close attention to pace—too fast and people will give up and go elsewhere. Too slow and the energy will drain away along the roadside. It is my experience that very often the slowest can go faster than they think they can, if they are encouraged to do so in the right way.

8

Stage 3—The Sacred Centre

Thanks be to God for thin places and safe arrivals;
help me, Holy Spirit, to encounter you afresh.

When asked the question, "What makes a pilgrimage different from a long-distance walk?", my answer would normally include an encounter with "the other", the divine. This is sometimes termed the "Sacred Centre" of the pilgrimage—although it may not be something which can be pinned down to one moment or one location.

The first time I visited Palestine/Israel was for a familiarization tour for people considering leading pilgrim groups in the future. For many years, I had resisted going, feeling sure that I would find no spiritual benefit in overcrowded sites vying for credibility as the authentic locations of different biblical events. When I did go, however, I found that day by day my preconceived notions were gently eroded—usually in surprising ways and at places which I might have deemed overcommercialized! Perhaps if pilgrimage has taught me anything it is to realize that God enjoys nothing more than breaking down our misconceptions and prejudices. Against this has to be set the possibility of disappointment, which may be another reason people choose not to visit significant holy sites: "What if I feel nothing?" As part of that first visit to the Holy Land in 2015, we walked the "Via Dolorosa" (a route through the old city of Jerusalem which seeks to recapture the walk of Jesus from his trial to the cross, with stations along the way for reflection). My journal from the week records the event thus: "Not the experience I had hoped for—would have liked to do the walk in silence. The whole thing took too long (including a stop for coffee and apple strudel!). Some meaningful moments, especially in the courtyard outside the Church of the Holy Sepulchre, but nothing inside to inspire really. Sorry." I'm not sure to whom I was apologizing! Perhaps the experience (or lack of it) provides a helpful reminder that God is indeed bigger and wilder than our imaginings, our itineraries and our expectations, and that all spiritual practices, including pilgrimage, are only tools by which we may encounter the uplift of the Spirit's wings, or we may not. The quest for the God of surprises is not like painting-by-numbers; it's much more exciting than that!

With all that as an opening disclaimer, I do believe that place is significant in pilgrimage and in life, perhaps to varying degrees depending on our own life story and personality. For many, the place where they were born continues to represent "home" until they die—even if they left it many years before (sometimes especially then). Others have fewer roots and move through life without that strong attachment to geographical origin, but often finding special places along the way. I think of the little hamlet on the Welsh coast where I spent many childhood holidays: if I close my eyes I can hear the lapping of the water on the shore, the cry of the oystercatchers, the rustling of the wind in the oak wood, I can smell the salt (and the seaweed), and I know that particular, precise location holds something special for me. So now does the bolt hole we have in the Scottish Highlands, where a sense of relationship with the soil of our garden is powerful, where the daily clues to the turning of the year's wheel are noticed in trees, plants, birds and creatures and where the ever-changing light on the mountains restores and extends my soul. Place holds memory—not only our own memories but a history of memory which is somehow stored in a particular location. When I stepped onto the Via Ignatia during a pilgrimage following St Paul's second missionary journey through Greece, I was completely overwhelmed by the sense that I was treading the same ground that he had trodden.

A Celtic approach to spirituality will often speak of "thin places", where heaven and earth seem almost to touch, where the division between the kingdom of God and the kingdoms of this world feel thin. This idea of the spirituality of place may run counter to our understanding that God is everywhere and that all places are sacred; however, it's not an "either/or" but a "both/and" experience. Feeling is key here; it is neither logical nor scientific—but human beings are much more than logic and science. Most of the well-known pilgrimage destinations I have visited have this quality—Lindisfarne, Iona, Ninian's Cave or, further afield, Bethlehem or Peter's burial site in Rome. Other pilgrims will want to include different places.

A key site for Jewish pilgrims, and for many Christians too, is the "Western Wall", that still-standing stretch of wall in the Old City of Jerusalem which formed part of the Second Temple, built by Herod the Great on the site of Solomon's Temple between 516 BC and AD 70. It is a highly sensitive site, not least because of its close physical proximity to the important Muslim pilgrimage site, the "Noble Sanctuary" (known to Jews as "Temple Mount"). This raises a critical question for pilgrims; can it be acceptable to visit such sites when their past history and their present experience are sadly steeped in contention and competition, even violence and blood? Perhaps the only appropriate approach is to tread very lightly: to surrender any sense of a "right" to be there at all, to comply with whatever religious restrictions are enforced, however these may grate against our own practices (e.g. the covering of the head for men and the restricted access available to women) and most of all to hold in mind the words of the psalmist, "Pray for the peace of Jerusalem" (Psalm 122:6). To describe the politics of Jerusalem as complex is a gross understatement and it is not my task here to try to unravel the many injustices of a tragic history.

My own visits to the Western Wall have been instructive; on my first visit Andrew and I walked to the wall just as dusk was falling on a Friday, in other words, at the start of the Sabbath. All around us Jews of every age and gender were hurrying, in some cases, running, to be at the wall as Sabbath began. Teenagers were dressed up, their faces full of joy and expectancy—this was where they wanted to be, where they would meet their friends, as well as offering their prayers; families rushed together, little children hurtling along in pushchairs. Older men and women moved more slowly, but with no less zeal in their faces. At this particularly holy hour, non-Jews were requested not to approach the wall at all, so we stood to the side, awed and impressed by this tidal wave of devotion as the moon rose and the courtyard was bathed in soft light and the murmuring of prayer. At other times, I have been able to walk right up to the wall (in the smaller, women's zone) and touch the stone, hearing the whispered and wailed prayers going on all around me, and, somehow, I caught a sense that the stones themselves are also exuding prayer and the hope of peace. Doves, sparrows and swallows cling to the wall (they've clearly read Psalm 84 and know they have a role to play here); between the stones are tiny rolls of paper, the prayers and hopes of countless petitioners over the years. Most memorable of all was being in Jerusalem during Holy Week in a year when Passover fell at the same time. On the Thursday (coinciding for us with Maundy Thursday), Jews gathered at the wall for the High Priestly blessing, loudly amplified so that all could hear. The courtyard and surrounding flights of steps were packed; we later heard that there were around 100,000 Jews present, many weeping and loudly lamenting the loss of the Temple. The ancient prayer of lament is being rediscovered in our day—it is not a prayer of moaning but a recognition of loss, that not all is right with the world and that God is big enough to hear our cries. We don't have to pretend that everything is fine! The Western Wall, is, I suggest, the most intense focus of lament in the world and a visit there might appropriately leave any pilgrim with a heart a little more broken but still hopeful.

The Bible is a narrative about places: some physical and identifiable still today, others mystical, spiritual or perhaps a mixture of all of these. The story of Adam and Eve's displacement from the Garden of Eden becomes the backdrop of the entire drama of salvation—when and how will we as a human race ever find our way back, our way home? Hebrews 13:14 once more: "For here we have no lasting city, but we are looking for the city that is to come." Throughout the Hebrew scriptures, the thread of displacement, or the fear of it, is crucial. Still today, displacement is a critical issue as thousands of people across the world either choose or are forced into migration for economic or political reasons. A question which I don't attempt to answer in this book, but which warrants all our attention, is how migration relates to pilgrimage. If a refugee is also a pilgrim, we must leave behind any notion of pilgrimage as a frothy optional extra for the wealthy or the spiritually elite—for many it is rather to be found in the grit of survival.

Within the larger context of place and displacement, some individual places develop significance, a fact borne out by the testimonies of many who seek asylum whilst still longing for "home". I find it fascinating to trace the story of particular places known to us from the Bible narrative, such as Bethel, named by Jacob in his own life as a pilgrim (see Chapter 1). At times, Bethel seems to have the status of a "thin place" both for Abram, returning in Genesis 13:3 "to the place where he had made an altar at the first; and there Abram called on the name of the LORD", and later for Jacob (Genesis 35:1). Were these journeys early pilgrimages to a sacred spot after both men had made mistakes in their relationships and dealings? Later Bethel becomes a place of wisdom and discernment (Judges 4:5; 20:18) before, sadly ending up as a place of idolatry; there are more references to this phase of its life than any other. In 1 Kings 12:29–30, King Jeroboam sets up calves of gold in Bethel and Dan (surely he should have known better; golden calves do not have a great track record in Jewish history). He sacrifices to them there and the rot sets in—by the time of Jesus it seems that Bethel has disappeared. It is a rot to which we should pay attention, for the threat which is always bubbling away alongside the exploration of pilgrimage is that of idolatry—a route or a destination, a person or a practice, a church or even a particular pew becomes first in our hearts, rather than the God to which all seek to point.

As I noted in Chapter 1, Jacob's experience at Bethel in Genesis 28 was, perhaps, the "Sacred Centre" of his entire life:

> Then Jacob woke from his sleep and said, 'Surely the LORD is in this place—and I did not know it!' And he was afraid, and said, 'How awesome is this place! This is none other than the house of God, and this is the gate of heaven.' (28:16–17)

This is perhaps the trickiest aspect of leading a pilgrimage, for how can any leader know where and when people are going to encounter God? The whole idea of saying on Wednesday morning, "This is the sacred centre of our pilgrimage" is surely doomed. Pilgrimage can never be a kind of bear-hunt to track God down; indeed, as we have noted already, post-Reformation Protestant opposition to pilgrimage was made partly on the grounds that God is everywhere, and it is not necessary to travel to find God. With a group today, all I can do is expect the unexpected, perhaps open the thinking of pilgrims to be attentive to God and make sure that we allow enough time for to God to do whatever God may want to do. God is the wild goose of Celtic symbolism, not to be constrained by my ideas or timetable.

As we might expect, sacred centres happen throughout the Bible story, many of them the subjects of later art, music and poetry. Hagar at the spring of water (Genesis 16:7) or the bush in the wilderness (Genesis 21:15); Moses at his wilderness bush (Exodus 3:2–6); Elijah at Horeb (1 Kings 19:12); Isaiah in the Temple (Isaiah 6:1–8). These are stories of people whose lives were changed when they experienced God in these places. In the Bible, theophanies are not merely about having a wonderful experience of God and going home feeling blessed—we do God a disservice if that is the aim of our worship or our wanderings. These are tales of life-changing encounters to do with survival and vocation, faithfulness and service. Artistic impressions of these stories don't feature cushions, roses and chocolate; venturing to the sacred centre may need courage.

Jesus too had some sacred centres in his life on earth, as did the disciples. Luke in his pilgrimage Gospel records many of them; the manger in Bethlehem (2:7); the shepherds in the fields (2:8); the moment of revelation in the temple to Simeon and to Anna (2:30,38); Simon Peter after the miraculous catch of fish (5:8); the storm on the Sea of Galilee (8:25); transfiguration on a mountain top (9:29); perhaps even being laid in the tomb (23:53) and more, right through to that meal in Emmaus (24:30). Such moments may bring joy but may also bring fear; as the writer to the Hebrews reminds us, "It is a fearful thing to fall into the hands of the living God" (10:31). Later events continue in the same vein: Paul on the road to Damascus (Acts 9); John on the island of Patmos (Revelation 1). Sacred encounter lies at the heart of Christian discipleship.

Centuries of Christian history bear out the same experience with cases too many to number, and it is still within the gracious nature of God to appear to us today, to tap us on the shoulder, to stop us in our tracks, to move us to tears. How we react to such moments may also be what defines us in life as pilgrims rather than tourists. These are the moments when we put away the guidebook or the camera in order to be fully present. We might do things which normally we wouldn't do—kiss the rock, take off our shoes, kneel on the ground, plunge our hands or feet—or our whole bodies—into water. It's a time to stop chattering and be quiet, or maybe to sing. Of course, you don't have to be "on" a pilgrimage to experience God closely, but perhaps something about the liminality, the insecurity, the vulnerability of being on the road (whether or not that is a physical road) sensitizes us to the Spirit. Our daily lives are generally full of stuff: material things on which our comfort and sustenance depend and to which we become accustomed. Pilgrimage can help us to regain the way of seeing which doesn't just look "at" these objects or activities, but which looks "through" them and discerns the spiritual reality behind or within the physical one. Again, the writer to the Hebrews captures it all so well, writing in Chapters 8 and 9 of the symbols which merely shadow the reality. So often our world gets this the wrong way round, seeing what is physical as "real" and what is spiritual as unimportant. Pilgrims learn a more excellent way.

—

One of the places I have been on pilgrimage which has affected me profoundly is St Ninian's Cave on the Galloway coast; in these lines I try to capture something of what a thin place can mean. It came together with the beautiful tune "Highwood" in mind:

A hymn for St Ninian's Cave—11 August 2017

> This is the place of ancient revelation,
> this is the place where saints have knelt and prayed.
> This is the place of blessing for this nation,
> the place where, now, our prayers and vows are made.
>
> Here, in this place, we feel the Spirit blowing,
> here, in this place, we sense that God is near.
> Here, in this place, the cloud of wild unknowing
> parts, to reveal the love which casts out fear.

Breathe in this place, the Spirit's timeless caring,
grieve in this place, for those you held so dear.
Sing in this place, of joy in love and sharing;
laugh and lament, for all of life is here.

This place is blessed by pilgrimage and presence;
this place is washed by oceans of God's grace.
This place invites our spirits' deepest longing
to live for Christ, in this and every place.

9

Stage 4—Endings and beginnings

Thanks be to God that every journey's end is also a beginning; help me, Jesus Christ, to set my face to travel onward with you. Amen.

How do you deal with endings? Whether it's coming to the end of a book we have enjoyed, completing a term of service in a particular role at church or at work, moving house or changing jobs, the breakdown of a relationship or another experience of rejection, we all experience endings in our lives; some we celebrate, some we scarcely notice, some cause us great grief. Perhaps the hardest endings we face in life are those which involve the death of someone we love. The death of an elderly or fading parent, even if long anticipated, can feel like the end of an era; the untimely death of a partner, spouse or friend tears our life into shreds and we wonder how to keep going; the tragic death of a child or young person casts us into a pit of loss and questions. When our son, Peter, died by suicide in 2012 at the age of 18, Andrew, Tim and I found ourselves in a dark, steep-sided valley—the valley of the shadow of death. So much came to an end in Peter's death—so many hopes, possibilities, expectations, longings, which I explore more in the next chapter, a pilgrimage of grief.

There is a tension around the idea of endings within the Christian faith, and within pilgrimage too. We know that there is an ultimate ending, a final destination towards which we are travelling—that same verse from Hebrews (13:14) points towards it: "For here we have no lasting city, but we are looking for the city that is to come." The expectation is clearly that one day we will arrive at that city. In the meantime, we are constantly on the journey, always travelling, changing day by day. Yet within this journey there are endings to be faced and worked through—perhaps one of the purposes of the journey is to teach us how to deal with endings, so that we will be prepared for the final end?

The group pilgrimages I have led have always had clear destinations in mind, but even so it may not be obvious when the pilgrimage itself has ended—is it when we reach that destination, or when, after spending some time there, we disperse and return to "normal" life? The fourth and final stage in my simple pilgrimage shape used to be "Return Transformed"—I would encourage pilgrims on our final day to consider how the journey had changed them and what they needed to hold onto from the whole adventure (and possible, what they needed to forget too!). The Christian gospel offers the perpetual challenge to be transformed, whether or not we think in terms of pilgrimage. But there is something about a journey, something about putting one foot in front of the other for days (or hours, or even minutes) which feeds renewal. A combination of intentionality, living lightly, undergoing transition, encountering God . . . these factors lead naturally to development, to new perspectives, to altered priorities, to quickened resolve. We read in 2 Corinthians 5:17: "So if anyone is in Christ, there is a new creation: everything old has passed away; see, everything has become new!" Through our pilgrimage we begin to see differently and to find a different viewpoint from which to make choices and form opinions—we inevitably do "return transformed".

However, over the years, my emphasis for this final stage has itself been transformed—now I focus more on the idea that "the end of every journey is the beginning of the next". It's not clearcut or straightforward—is anything in life?—instead, it's important not to put ourselves under too much pressure and the idea of being attentive pilgrims to life's journey 24/7 might be rather exhausting. Can't we just relax and recover from this journey before we set off again? Of course we can—and it's important that we do, but maybe it is still worth holding onto the idea that a few days or weeks or months of rest can, in itself, be another journey—into God, into stillness, into the Spirit. The end of a group pilgrimage can be hard—some will be dreading returning to an empty house after days of camaraderie on the road (others will be longing for it). Rhythm (explored in Chapter 5) helps us again here; the turning of the earth creates a rhythm of light and darkness and reminds us on a daily basis that the end of one journey is the beginning of another; "The sun that bids us rest is waking our friends beneath the western sky" as the hymn puts it.[24]

The Bible has many stories of endings of all sorts—maybe we think of Noah's flood in Genesis 6-9 where God seems to switch the world off and on again, as many of us do when computers go wrong! The rather strange writings of "The Teacher" in Ecclesiastes (7:8) include the phrase, "Better is the end of a thing than its beginning", which may have a certain wisdom to it, but as verse 3 of the passage says that "Sorrow is better than laughter" we might take note that the philosophy of Ecclesiastes is usually better taken in small doses. Many of the chapters of the Gospels are taken up in dealing with the final days of Jesus' life—and John devotes a large chunk to the farewell teachings at the Last Supper. In the beautiful narration of the two disciples on the Emmaus Road on the first Easter Sunday evening (Luke 24:13-35), we meet characters who feel as if everything they valued has come to an end with Jesus' death. But by the end of the chapter, they have discovered the most dramatic new beginning of all, for Jesus' death and resurrection is the extreme illustration of the end of every journey being the beginning of the next. The apostle Paul also shares words of wisdom and admonition when he says farewell to church leaders in Ephesus, and at the end of his final letter to the church at Corinth (2 Corinthians 13:11) he writes: "Finally, brothers and sisters, farewell. Put things in order, listen to my appeal, agree with one another, live in peace; and the God of love and peace will be with you." More sound advice for times of parting.

The Methodist system of itinerancy for its ministers (which we looked at a little in Chapter 4) has built into it the need to deal with endings and beginnings several times in a lifelong ministry—not only for the minister and family, but for congregations too. This can be hard for all sides and, if not handled well, can cause hurt and pain. When we left the Caribbean in 2001 to return to ministry in the British Methodist Church, Andrew said that it felt as if 700 members of his family had died overnight—given the distance and cost of travelling (and the relatively scarce internet access at that time in the communities where we had lived), there was little likelihood that we would be able to maintain

---

[24] "The day thou gavest, Lord, is ended" by John Ellerton (*StF* 147).

relationships and friendships. Did we want to? In some ways of course we did, but in others, no. New ministers living constantly within the shadow of their predecessor may fail to flourish—not for nothing does the writer of Genesis advocate (2:24) that "a man leaves his father and his mother and clings to his wife" (and this applies equally to other roles and genders). For new relationships and situations to grow and develop well, there has to be a sense of ending, of farewell, of separation. When, at the end of one circuit appointment, Andrew warned people not to expect him to keep closely in touch, a woman asked him how he could possibly "cast off" people with whose lives he had been so closely connected for the previous five years. His response was to point out that he would not have been able to be so closely connected to them had he not "cast off" the ties of his previous appointment.

When I took the first, pilot, pilgrimage to Lindisfarne in 2014, I had chosen "Horizons" as the final day's word. We would, I had thought, ponder on how our social horizons had enlarged as we left this small band of people and returned to our wider world, and how, similarly, the tiny horizons of a little island would soon be expanded as we returned to the towns and cities of our homes. Thankfully, before sharing these words of very dubious wisdom with the group, I realized that it was not like that at all, in fact quite the reverse. No city or town has such an expansive horizon as a small island does—standing on the highest point of Lindisfarne, the Heugh, one can see for miles in every direction; oceans of possibility and hills of opportunity lie all around. The pilgrim needs to take something of that breadth of potential back into crowded streets, housing estates or full diaries. Is there also something here which can aid us in our walk into old age? For many, there is both the expectation and the experience that horizons will shrink as we become less mobile, less acute, less active, but a journey with a big and wild God surely doesn't have to end tamely? My father was already living with Parkinson's Disease when we moved to St Vincent in 1994, but my parents made the huge physical and financial effort to visit, three times in all. I will never forget the light shining in my father's eyes on the first evening of their first visit; "To think that I would ever stand on West Indian soil!" he said with wonder—as a lifelong cricket enthusiast, this was holy ground indeed! Although over the eight years which followed life was often difficult for them as his disease progressed, something of that sense of wonder and of connection stayed with them and their own horizons were broadened by the letters, prayers and practical action they took to continue a remote involvement not only in our family life, but in the life of the Methodist churches where we worshipped week by week. Despite reduced mobility, it is possible to live on a big map.

An important part of every pilgrimage I have led has been the time spent at the end on "re-entry". Berwick-upon-Tweed railway station has a very cosy waiting room on one of its platforms—and it has seen many emotions shared amongst pilgrims about to head both north and south after the taxi ride from Lindisfarne on the final day. I might begin by asking everyone to name someone they are looking forward to seeing again (including pets who often receive more votes than humans!); and we rejoice together in the relationships from which we have been cut off for some days, but which will give us pleasure when we return. There is a sense in which we have been blessed in order to be a blessing, in which we return not *with* gifts, for shopping is not generally a part of walking pilgrimage (although visits to the Holy Land will inevitably involve many forays into shops and stalls filled with olive wood carvings, spices and star-shaped jewellery) but *as* gifts. We do, however, take note of something to which Phil Cousineau first drew my attention when I read *The Art of Pilgrimage*. Under the heading "Bringing back the boon", he cautions against pilgrims returning to the bosom of their family or circle of friends with *too* many stories of what happened on the road. Even the most loving, patient companion may not really want to hear everything (again, a faithful dog is the best listener), so some of the wisdom learned on the journey need to be treated as the treasure it is and stored in the heart where it can reap dividends for the carrier over many years. Like Mary, there is great value in "pondering these things in our hearts" (Luke 2:19).

Secondly, I might ask the group to share one thing which they are not looking forward to on their return—a tricky encounter or decision, a pile of emails, a challenging relationship—and to commit to praying for each other over the coming days bearing those scenarios in mind. Sometimes we may have been deliberately not thinking about these challenges while on the road, and that may have been beneficial, but beneficial too is the courage to face them again whilst still in this liminal place, whilst the tang of the salty wind is still on our lips, or the aroma of incense still in our nostrils. Looked at in the light of our pilgrimage, they may take on a different hue, or we can recognize that the resources we have developed during the time apart have somehow equipped us to deal better with whatever we face.

Finally, because we may well have been somewhat introspective on our pilgrimage, attending to our own and others' spiritual and physical needs, but letting the rest of the world do as it may, I invite everyone to call to mind a situation further afield which troubles them and for which they want to pray. To embody this, we then turn physically from being a circle facing inwards to facing away from each other in myriad directions and offer ourselves as lights to shine in the wider world, praying that the Holy Spirit, the wild goose of God, will lead us into the next stage of our journey. Then, we board our trains—and that too is an essential part of the debrief; a slow decompression time when we can adjust, a buffer zone to avoid switching too quickly from one world to another—we want to avoid getting the bends. Some will write a journal on the way home, recording those treasures—including emotions—which they want to retain, or purging themselves of difficult times. A stone or a shell taken home may be a tangible reminder of this in coming days.

The Bible concludes with the assurance that, at the end, all things will be made new and will begin again:

> And the one who was seated on the throne said, 'See, I am making all things new.' Also he said, 'Write this, for these words are trustworthy and true.' Then he said to me, 'It is done! I am the Alpha and the Omega, the beginning and the end. (Revelation 21:5–6)

I'm not sure how that will work out, but I know there is great appeal in it. We all know the freshness and wonder of a new beginning—a clean page in a new exercise book; a newly decorated room, a new house or perhaps a new garden or patch of land waiting to be planted. For an artist, a blank canvas, a new piece of fabric, a block of marble. Does this appeal connect with something deeper inside us which knows we have messed up and need to start again? Rewind the tape, erase that sentence we said, that letter we wrote, that scenario in which we became ensnared? The good news of the gospel, of pilgrimage, is that transformation is always on offer and beyond every ending lies the possibility of new beginnings, for God is at our side, the bigger, wilder, pilgrim God.

EPILOGUE

A pilgrimage of grief

Before I close, I have set myself the task of applying all the history, theory and experience of pilgrimage which has filled these pages so far, to my own life; in particular to the journey of grief I have walked since the death of our son, Peter, by suicide, in July 2012. In other words, does it work? As I start, I wonder if I will find myself disagreeing with myself at times . . . ? I hope too that, whilst being intensely personal, this chapter might resonate with you as you consider your own challenges on the journey of life; can a mindset of being a pilgrim, seeking a bigger and wilder God, make a difference?

I begin this epilogue during Advent 2022. Advent is my favourite season of the year, and now it is being spent in my favourite place. Thanks to the wonderful gift of sabbaticals, which the Methodist Church offers to its ministers every seven years, Andrew and I are both spending three months based at our little cottage in the Scottish Highlands. Like Lindisfarne, for us this feels like a thin place; like Whithorn, wild beauty is on every side; like Jerusalem we are surrounded by mountains; like the holy family in Bethlehem we share our space with non-human companions; deer and sheep roam the hillsides around and occasionally seek to invade the garden, birdlife is manifold, from tiny wrens to majestic buzzards (a goldfinch has joined other garden birds on the feeders outside my window as I write), and our newest neighbours are beavers who have taken residence in the burn 50 feet away and are changing the landscape with remarkable speed! In many ways, this space has become for us the unexpected destination of peace and even happiness, and yet we are also still on a journey. Many of the headings I have used in earlier chapters need to be re-examined in the light of lived experience: direction, company, timing, destination, courage . . . how have these played out in my life and has any part of the journey been made easier, or more worthwhile, by seeing it as a pilgrimage?

Yesterday we climbed the small mountain closest to the cottage. It was a wonderful walk, filled with remarkable light as the sun broke through clouds and reflected off snow and ice on the higher slopes. Over the years, we have developed a good route to the summit, passing three cairns along the way, all of which give great views over the surrounding valleys and hills. Coming down, however, is a different matter—not wanting to retrace our entire route, we search every time for another descent—some are better than others! Yesterday was one of the worst; we started to drop too soon and found ourselves in the wrong valley, not at all where we expected to be. Confronted with a vast area of coniferous forest, some of which was harvested about five years ago and some of which is still growing (around the devastation caused by Storm Arwen in November 2021), we had an invidious choice—try to penetrate the impenetrable and descend through the living forest, or try to navigate the unnavigable and cross the hazardous wastes of tree stumps, broken branches, slippery mud and long-abandoned wire fences. We chose the latter, and we did reach home, but it was hard work. Scotland's "right to roam" policy means that very few areas are private, and it is almost impossible to trespass anywhere, but consequently there are far fewer paths and much more is left to the individual walker to find a path.

As we persevered, and knowing I was planning to start work on this chapter today, I reflected about the parallels with the journey of grief, and the differences. Grief is, I suggest, much more like walking in little-known, pathless areas than on well-trodden routes. There is not a clear and safe path through grief with colour-coded way markers by which you can decide how long to spend on the journey. The choices are often invidious, the terrain unwelcoming and unforgiving, the effort of travelling exhausting and wearisome. There may be those who suggest there is an "A to Z" of the territory of grief, and there are books and websites which offer travel instructions, suggesting a clear transition from one stage to the next. Most of these are now falling out of favour, and rightly so. Despite what others may say (often with the best of intentions), I don't believe there is anyone else who knows "exactly how you feel". We have to make our own path and when that is difficult, it doesn't mean that we are "doing it wrong" or have missed the smooth highway of survival which is just off to the left, if only we had noticed it. That smooth highway is an illusion; worse, a deception. The road through grief is tough.

That is not to say there is nothing to be learned or gained from others. I have said quite definitively (in Chapter 7) that the pilgrim is never alone—that we are always walking in the footsteps of those who have gone before and somehow as forerunners of those still to come. Does that not apply to the journey of grief? I think it does, I believe that the company of saints, the "cloud of witnesses", can offer us something, but we may need to be careful about our choice of companions and cautious about putting too much trust in them. After Peter died, we were given dozens of books; poems and reflections about death, medical analyses about suicide, personal accounts of survival, theological treatises about what it all means. Some I put away in a drawer for possible later reference—some of those are still there. A few I dipped into and wished I hadn't. (If you are now in the position of trying to support someone recently bereaved, I would suggest chocolate over a book.) There are two small pieces of wisdom, however, which did connect with me in those early days and which have been my travelling companions ever since; the first I read on a website (which I don't think I could find again) where a bereaved woman wrote, "I just want people to treat me normally, but I get so angry when they do." A brilliant summing up of the conflicting emotions of bereavement. The other came in the introduction to *Poppies and Snowdrops* in which a small section was devoted to parents whose child had died.[25] Wisely it pointed out that even two people as close as this and who share the same experience will need to grieve differently. Don't be exasperated with each other, it counselled, when one wants to sit all day staring into space and the other has energy to work or dig or clear out cupboards; allow each other to find a way through this devastation which works for them. Figures vary, but most surveys suggest that the divorce or separation rate for couples who have known the death of a child is very high; this was and remains helpful guidance.

---

[25] Andrew Pratt and Marjorie Dobson, *Poppies and Snowdrops: Resources for Times of Grief and Bereavement* (Peterborough: Inspire, 2006).

To be part of a wider community where everyone experiences grief at some point and where most people have devised routes to help them through it, can offer wisdom, comfort and strength—but it may not always be easy, especially in the early stages of disorientation, to sift through all the words to find what is most helpful. Particularly after the death of a second parent, those bereaved are often offered phrases such as "Your parents are together again now" in an effort to provide some comfort. I'm not sure on what authority such platitudes are spoken; I don't find anything quite so clear in scripture myself, although there are times when I long to believe it. Will I see Peter again in heaven? I don't know, but if not, I trust it will be better than that.

Yesterday, to our surprise (for this is a little-known area of the southern Highlands), at the summit of the mountain we saw footprints in the snow which were not our own. They came from a different direction and they left on another path; our routes never crossed each other but we knew that someone else had climbed this mountain we were on. That is always true. There are always others on the steep slopes of grief—maybe it would be a surprise to us to know how many, for it seems that our culture (even in church) expects us to spare the feelings of others by not talking about our heartbreak beyond a decent interval of perhaps (if they are being generous) a year. We have to make our own way, and it won't be the right way, because there isn't one. Death is wrong; the narrative of creation presented in the early chapters of Genesis suggest that death is not part of the original plan of life and later scriptures present the destruction of death as the primary focus of the work of Jesus. Yes, there may be times when death comes as a relief and yes, there are circumstances when it is possible to have a good death but ultimately "the city which is to come" for which we seek and to which we are heading will not contain death. Whilst being obscure about most things relating to what happens after death, the Bible is very clear on that; Isaiah 25:6–9 assures us that God "will swallow up death for ever" and Revelation 21:4 promises that "Death will be no more".

Over our years of walking together, Andrew and I have been lost many times. On one memorable occasion long ago in the Lake District, again in snowy conditions, we thought we had found footprints which might help us discover how to descend, only to realize (eventually) as we recognized the unusual shape of a pile of rocks, that they were our own footprints and we were going round in circles. The road of grief is not linear; if we are going round in circles, so be it—at least we are still moving, we have not given up the journey all together.

And what of timing and pacing on this journey of grief? Again, there is no guidebook telling us how long the expedition should take us (or if there is, please ignore it). Yesterday on the mountain I knew that, barring an accident, within three or four hours of leaving the summit, we would have returned home, we would be able to run a deep bath and light the log burner, we would be able to make a hot drink and know that, whilst our muscles still ached, the journey was over. In grief there are no such assurances—"How long will this go on?" is a heartfelt cry when feeling overwhelmed by weariness and heartbreak.

Reflecting thus is a salutary reminder to me that life is rarely tidy—and if there are places in this book where I have suggested that either pilgrimage or life can be neatly ordered under headings such as Departure, Journey, Encounter and Transformation, then please ignore them! Searching for a bigger and wilder God must mean abandoning an overriding desire for things to be neat and tidy. Whilst in some circumstances the departure into grief can be planned and prepared for, in others it can't and so the journey begins amidst shock and trauma. The principle of "Living lightly" does offer wisdom, however. Being wise enough to shed unnecessary responsibilities can help, as can packing new things into the baggage such as intentional space to grieve. Andrew and I had just begun a fortnight's holiday when Peter died, so there were, thankfully, no immediate commitments in the diary to be fulfilled or rearranged, but when the fortnight was over, we both decided to return to our normal roles, not as if nothing had happened, but because we couldn't face the prospect of sitting staring at a wall day after day. Within the busyness of our lives, however, Andrew's Friday day off became a precious time to allow our grief to come to the fore, to think and talk more about Peter, to watch the videos, look at the photos, reread the letters of condolence. Time away became important too, and each month for about six months we booked the sort of hotel bargain mini breaks in coastal retirement towns which are largely aimed at pensioners and which we might never have considered in "normal" times. Sometimes we were even able to raise a smile or a laugh, imagining how Peter would have reacted to our uncharacteristic behaviour! The pacing of the journey matters. Julie Hulme (mentioned in Chapter 5) offered another helpful idea about what might be carried on the journey; after I wrote in a letter to her that I only felt at peace when gardening, she responded with the suggestion that to incorporate small creative acts into each day might be a way to counter the despair. I have never found that paints or crayons produce what I imagine they might (the only year I had a good report for Art at school was the year I came to an arrangement with the teacher and spent the weekly lesson tidying and cleaning the cupboard and equipment), but writing, cooking, photography, gardening... all these and more have helped and do help. Now in this beautiful little corner of the Scottish Highlands, noticing shapes of branches, colours of berries and textures of leaves in the garden and bringing them indoors in jugs is remarkably healing.

Everyone has different ways of describing the ongoing journey—the image of learning to live *around* the chasm which has opened up in our lives is one I find helpful. Sometimes my thoughts or experiences might take me to the very edge of that chasm, and I peer into the abyss for a day or longer. At other times, I find myself on paths which are further away from it, but I always know it is there. Some of the qualities I describe as "Pilgrim graces" in Chapter 5 have indeed offered grace to me along the way. Despite the natural tendency I have already described to shy away from encounter, I have realized that when it comes to bereavement, and particularly bereavement by suicide, there is a massive swell of unspoken grief and pain under the surface of many lives which needs to break, and the shores of other people's experiences might offer that relief. The roles I have had within the Methodist Church over these years of grief have given me many platforms for speaking to groups of people, from invitations to preach on Sunday mornings to wider gathered events for training or fellowship. At many, I have spoken about Peter's death and its impact on our lives; it is costly and sometimes I ask myself why I do it. Part of the answer lies in the fact that on all the dozens of occasions when I have done so, there has always been at least one person who has spoken to me afterwards about their own experience of bereavement by suicide, often including words such as, "I haven't told anyone else it was suicide", "I don't talk about this at church", "I've never told anyone this before". Others speak about their fears for a family member or friend, very often a young man. Taboos around mental health and suicide are being eroded, but there is still a long way to go. My hope is that speaking out and allowing encounters such as these to happen is part of that process. It is also a risk, and there have been a few comments after such occasions which make me realize why many prefer to keep their stories to themselves; I suppose the worst (but one I find it impossible to forget) was the woman who commented, "You must ask yourself where you went wrong as a mother." Oh yes, my dear, you can be sure I do. Even when my head assures me that it is not a healthy direction in which to go, my heart asks me that very question, and weeps. There is really no need at all for anyone else to play the guilt card when speaking to survivors of bereavement by suicide—we are already holding it in spades.

Perhaps that unthinking comment serves as a reminder that we all need to exercise more attentiveness to the words we choose! I would want to liberate everyone from the feeling that they need to think of the "right thing to say" to a bereaved person, for I maintain that no one else can, by their words, their actions or even their silence, put things right; the wrong done by death is far too great and deep for that, but there are certainly comments which can be avoided, and a little forethought does not go amiss. When the pilgrim band from Methodist Women in Britain visited the beautiful crusader church at Bethesda in Jerusalem, dedicated to St Anne, the mother of Mary the mother of Jesus, a kindly "White Father" officiating at the church briefly addressed us and, seeing we were a women's group, exhorted us all to teach our children to "love the Lord" as Mary had done for Jesus, with the strong implication being that then all would be well. I found myself kicking against this, wanting to shout, "There are no guarantees"—more helpful in my view is the honest, if painful, approach of Simeon who tells Mary that "a sword will pierce your own soul too" (Luke 2:35).

Sharing our experiences and our emotions means displaying our vulnerability, something which many of us find it hard to do. Over the past decade, I have come to understand something of the strength which lies in weakness and have become more convinced that rather than good leadership requiring iron control and inviolability, there is much grace and love to be revealed when leaders are willing to be vulnerable. Despite my zealous (overzealous?) attention to detail when planning pilgrimages, I have been known to make mistakes, some of which are here related. On every occasion, the group has risen to the consequent difficulties with good humour and kindness—almost as if they welcomed the opportunity to glimpse my human fallibility! More seriously, those times when I have been overwhelmed with emotion myself, whilst trying to lead others, have also brought forth grace, support and often personal testimony which simply wouldn't have surfaced had I kept my emotions firmly in check. In a Communion service at the Garden Tomb in Jerusalem, my co-leader, Elizabeth Rundle, had invited me to give the brief address which, it has to be said, was more about death than about resurrection, but which came from somewhere deep within. I held it together and sat down again afterwards with no little relief. Elizabeth then led us through a beautiful Communion liturgy which included remembrance of "those we have loved but see no longer", and the internal dam on my emotions burst with a literal flood of tears. The outpouring of love and solidarity from fellow pilgrims which followed matched the strength of my grief and forged lasting bonds of friendship and mutuality. Being accepted by a bigger and wilder God gets rid of some of the filters I have applied to life in the past.

Courage for the journey has already played a significant part in my description of life as a pilgrim, and it relates to my life as a bereaved mother on a daily basis. With roots in the Latin word for the heart, *cor*, courage is both an emotion and a decision but also, I believe, a gift. Not a gift like a perfume which can be sprayed on; it is more like a scooter which has to be ridden to prove its worth. The courage to keep going day after day is not to be taken for granted, and there have been some days when it has been hard to find. In the early days of bereavement, I so dreaded the question, "How are you?" (unless it was being asked in a private space by a close friend who really wanted to hear the answer, whatever that might be). In the years which have followed I have sought for a better way to greet people I encounter at church or in the shops who have been recently bereaved, for I know how easily that facile question comes out unless we have armed ourselves with alternatives. My best offering is, "It's good to see you" which acknowledges something of the courage which has led to the griever being able to leave the safety of their home at all, and also underlines their continuing worth and value. Doing normal things can be so hard when carrying the heavy weight of grief, once described to me by a friend as being as exhausting as running uphill all the time. Whilst everyday normal rhythms can be a tremendous help, for all the reasons examined previously, the expectation of a rhythm can be a burden when our resources are low. Do I have to do this? Does it matter whether or not I get dressed, make a meal, say my prayers, go to church . . . ? Overall I look back and recognize that for me, approaching life with my unique set of peculiarities, rhythm has generally been helpful, at least at its most basic level—keep breathing, keep getting out of bed, keep putting one foot in front of the other, keep opening the Bible and trying to pray. God is gracious, and even on this demanding road there are epiphanies and sacred centres, but I have learned that epiphanies with a big wild God are not experiences which leave me feeling warm and peaceful, or not all of them are. Some of the times when I have been most aware of the nearness of God have left me feeling drained and broken, yet with the courage to limp on.

In 2007, when Peter was 12 and Tim 17, we spent a fun-filled few weeks camping in parts of continental Europe—Bratislava, Prague, Vienna and Berlin. This last city, quite well known to Andrew, who had spent time there many years ago, captivated us all. We spent one harrowing morning at the Holocaust Memorial Museum and then wandered around the Memorial to the Murdered Jews of Europe designed by architect Peter Eisenman and Buro Happold. This open-air memorial is sited over nearly 20,000 square meters and consists of 2,711 concrete slabs which rise up from a sloping piece of land. In some places, the slabs are knee-high or less, in others they tower above the visitor, the highest reaching 4.7 metres. Although they are arranged in rows, the angles between the rows are slightly askew and this, along with the sloping ground, leads, intentionally, to a feeling of disorientation. From around the age of eleven, Peter was obsessional about the colour orange and was usually dressed in something of that colour. One of my favourite photographs of Peter was taken that day as he wandered silently and pensively around the memorial, a small flash of orange amidst the great grey slabs. He loved the photo too, and we had a huge poster made of it for his thirteenth birthday—it still hangs in our bedroom, and as I look at it, I can feel something of the liminality which the designers of the memorial intended to convey and which Peter's life seemed to absorb and reflect. A sense that the ground cannot be fully relied upon, that life can suddenly move from seeming under control to being overwhelming, that in the end, each of us is alone, at least in some respects. Resisting the impulse to settle down, to tidy up, to have everything under control but instead learning, however imperfectly, about liminality, and learning to recognize and even embrace it in my own life and in the lives of others have been valuable tools for the journey. I only wish I had had a more nuanced approach to what is important in life when Peter was still around to discuss it. Perhaps one of his fears was that he would never get life under control in the way he wanted to; perhaps we all need to let go of that ambition? However stable we may feel our circumstances to be, they can be rocked at any time. Valuing, rather than fearing, transition, uncertainty, liminality and change may make the difference between surviving and going under.

Perhaps that leads me to the question I hardly dare address but know that I must. Does everything I have said about the need for pilgrims to stick to the journey and not give up before the destination is reached, mean that, in some sense, suicide is a failure to be a pilgrim? Perhaps if I were being asked the question in a theoretical setting, I might agree with that logic, but this is a personal reflection on the journey of grief after the suicide of a greatly loved son, Peter. The parameters are different.

Around the time of Peter's death, a word being used widely in the World Federation of Methodist and Uniting Church Women, of which I am a part, was the South African word *bambelela*, meaning "Never give up". I was asked to lead a residential retreat for women in Cornwall in 2013 based on this word. During the week, I gradually realized that these neatly scripted sessions didn't match up to the truth of lived experience and the final talk had to be rewritten with more nuance. There are times in life when giving up is the right thing to do. Sometimes it's trivial; being willing to return a book to the library unfinished when you realize it's not saying anything to you. Sometimes it's economically damaging; resigning from a post which you know is eating away at your soul. Sometimes it's unpopular; stepping down from a role at church which isn't working out, even though there is no one else to fill it. Sometimes it's a matter of life and death, such as leaving an abusive relationship. There are many times in our lives when "giving up" is the strongest, bravest course to take. To the woman who, after hearing my story, tried to counsel me by saying that Peter's suicide was "alright for him but hard for the family" I want to shout a resounding "NO!" Neither she, nor I, have any idea of the depths of despair which Peter must have known. Depths which, tragically, are experienced by the estimated 700,000 people around the world who take their own lives each year, and by the much greater number (possibly 20 times that) who make suicide attempts.[26]

Peter's funeral took place less than a week after his death, on Friday, 13 July 2012. Perhaps no one else had wanted a slot on this "unlucky" date—I don't think the associations of the date registered with me until much later. Before a service of thanksgiving for his life at St Andrew's Methodist Church, Slough, attended by around 400 people, we held a cremation at which I touched upon how Peter might have felt, suggesting that in experiencing the shock and grief at the void his death opened in our lives we might be closest to where Peter himself had been at times in the previous few years. I finished by saying:

> Peter chose to bring his life to an end before he began to slip into something both he and anyone who loved him would have found intolerable. For that I believe we can, and must, be thankful, however much it hurts now and always will. I could not have wished him to suffer mentally in this way any longer. He asks us to accept that he could not find peace and appeals to us all, 'Let me go, please'. Today needs to be about letting him go; not into the dark unknown, as he may have thought himself in his final, confused state, but into the arms of God, into the light which pushes back the darkness completely and which frees the mind.

That phrase, "pushing back the darkness" was something I had occasionally spoken of with Peter, as it was a need I was aware of to a lesser extent in my own life. I was not a stranger to the sense of being

---

[26] https://www.who.int/campaigns/world-suicide-prevention-day/2022, accessed 10 February 2023.

overwhelmed, of being unequal to the demands of life, of wanting to hide and not face the commitments in the diary, and Peter found it both surprising and comforting to know that. We spoke about the need to dig deeply into inner resources and he, as a skilled actor, learned how to do this with flair. The shock of his college friends at the news of his suicide was a measure of his success in overcoming anxieties and living life to the full. But to do this day in day out is wearing; in the end the cost was too great for Peter and he had to end the journey. A well-known radio presenter whose son ended his own life in his early twenties used words to which I often return: "He stayed as long as he could."

One legacy of Peter's death for my own spirituality has been a much deeper exploration and appreciation of darkness. This began when I noticed for the first time the words of Isaiah 45:3; "I will give you the treasures of darkness and riches hidden in secret places, so that you may know that it is I, the LORD the God of Israel, who call you by your name." That wonderfully evocative phrase, "treasures of darkness" lodged in my thinking; could it be that darkness is not unremittingly gloomy? Around the same time, we came across Barbara Brown Taylor's book *Learning to Walk in the Dark* (which uses the same Bible text as an inspiration) and read avidly of a new and different approach to darkness, seeing it as a natural part of the rhythm of life, not the evil for which it is so often used as a metaphor. In the past few years, much more attention has been paid to the nurturing, mystical, creative, healing aspects of darkness, and I could write at least another chapter on that alone. Suffice it for now to say that discovering that both darkness and silence can be the arena of God's activity has been redemptive and life-giving. Again, I wish I had mined for these treasures before I did—whilst recognizing that perhaps I needed to experience the loss and grief of Peter's death in order to be ready to give up my Sunday school theology of darkness and light and make way for a bigger, wilder God.

When planning a group pilgrimage, I endeavour to fit the walking into daylight hours for all sorts of common-sense reasons. The few occasions when something has taken place in the darkness stand out: the candlelit outdoor labyrinth which a member of the team organized during a pilgrimage weekend at Cliff College; or reading Psalm 104 by torchlight in a small garden at the end of a day, especially verses 19 and

20: "You have made the moon to mark the seasons; the sun knows its time for setting. You make darkness, and it is night, when all the animals of the forest come creeping out." Perhaps most memorable of all was the night a small group of pilgrims set out at 10 p.m. from our warm comfy hostelry on Lindisfarne in the hope of seeing the predicted meteor shower and ending up lying flat on our backs on the grass by the harbour, watching shooting stars to the accompaniment of seals singing! Treasures of darkness indeed.

Darkness still has its menace and its challenges, of course. At the site in Palestine/Israel known as "Gallicantu", where the apostle Peter's denial of Jesus and Jesus's subsequent imprisonment in the High Priest's house is marked, I descended with a large group of pilgrims the many steps into a dark pit which could have been the overnight cell where Jesus was held. Embedded in the wall is a plaque bearing the words of Psalm 88, which, using a phone to give light, someone read aloud; perhaps Jesus also recited this psalm during his incarceration. In the translation used at Gallicantu, the final words of the psalm are rendered, "My only friend is darkness". On that first occasion, surrounded by physical darkness I wept for the inner darkness I had experienced, for the sense in which perhaps Peter welcomed darkness as a friend, and to understand that something of these agonies was well known to and fully understood by Jesus himself.

In the previous chapter, I reflected a little on endings and beginnings and how it can be difficult to deal with unwanted endings in our lives, but it needs to be done. Literature tells us stories of those, like Miss Havisham in *Great Expectations*, who deny the reality of endings and live a life of make-believe; we may know such characters in our own lives too. It's easy to see why they would behave in this way—to come up against the intractable finality of death is something from which we all shrink. I have found it helpful, sometimes, to reflect on the timelessness of God or the vastness of creation. In an eternal perspective, what I am facing, huge as it seems to me now, may lose a little of its horror. Out walking, this time descending Cadair Idris in Snowdonia, not long after Peter's death, I watched a great bird flying effortlessly amidst the heights which had been so challenging for us to climb and I thought of the age of those rocks and felt very small. Feeling small is good, for when one sets a human life span against the life of a mountain, whether the life is 18 or

80 years long, it seems relatively unimportant. Or maybe I recall the faith of so many saints over the ages who have clung to the belief that, in the end, all will be well, that "This too will pass". However the destination is to be understood, holding onto the idea that there is one is something which keeps me going. There will come a day when the pilgrimage of grief will be over, for "he will wipe every tear from their eyes. Death will be no more; mourning and crying and pain will be no more, for the first things have passed away" (Revelation 21:4).

At times, the pilgrimages I have led have included intentional space to reflect on loss and grief. The remote beach on the Galloway coast, the site of St Ninian's Cave, is a location which seems to lend itself to this. I gather the group around and begin by inviting suggestions of biblical stories which feature beaches and caves, and, amongst others, we might talk about Elijah (1 Kings 19), about Jesus cooking breakfast for the disciples after his Resurrection (John 21), or about Paul saying farewell to the Ephesian elders on the beach at Miletus (Acts 20). What blew my mind the first time I realized it was that Ninian, who lived in the fourth century AD, is closer in time to Jesus and Paul, closer even in time to Elijah, than he is to us! So we ponder this incredible chain of witness which has run throughout the history of God's interaction with humanity and give thanks, not just for these heroes of the past, but for the individuals we have loved but see no longer, who were also links in the chain which has brought us to this place and this moment in time.

With the waves breaking on the shore not far from where we are seated and the salty spray of the sea acting like incense to our worship, it is a moving and powerful time and I am glad for a group of people with whom I am safe enough to talk about Peter and to weep. After this time of sharing in May 2022 with a wonderful group of women who had, because of Covid, waited more than two years to make this pilgrimage, Gillian, my co-leader for the expedition, gave us all half walnut shells, symbolic of the little coracles in which some of the early saints set off on pilgrimage. As we held them quietly in our hands, we made our own pledge to God and then launched them into the sea, into the hands of a big, wild God:

I have rested here a while,
been reacquainted with your peace, have felt your love.
Now, as I push my coracle onto unknown waters
watch over me, be my guide and my strength. Amen.[27]

---

[27] A Lindisfarne Prayer by Ruth Sprague.

APPENDIX

Pilgrimage on the doorstep

If pilgrimage is to be a resource for the whole Church, it must be broader than organized group pilgrimages to distant lands, or even the kind of walking pilgrimages with which I have been involved. It needs to be accessible to all and affordable by all, and I believe it can be. Living life with a pilgrim spirit is not restricted to the economically well-off or to the physically fit.

A few ideas follow of how pilgrimage might be made available on anyone's doorstep—these are by no means exhaustive but perhaps they may trigger ideas for your situation or locality.

The first P: Place

Pilgrimage tends to be associated with particular places, so I begin there, wherever "there" may be for you. It is important to recognize the significance of sacred places, sometimes called "thin places" where something "other" may be experienced. Locations where, perhaps because of what has happened there in the past, or because of the prayers which have been offered there for centuries, there is a sense of God's closeness, of the division between heaven and earth being thin. My husband, Andrew, recently fell into conversation with a couple on Lindisfarne who had never been there before, knew nothing of the history or spirituality of the island but confessed to having experienced "a weird feeling" since they had arrived. In pilgrimage, we hold onto the holiness of place, whether that is for individuals or collectively. But place, whilst important, is not everything. The more we attempt to tie God down to a building or a location, the more God will spring up elsewhere.

A number of famous sites have been mentioned already, but there are thousands more and some of them may be near to where you live. Methodist Heritage encourages pilgrimage to their four key sites (the Old Rectory at Epworth in Lincolnshire; the New Room (aka John Wesley's Chapel) Bristol; Wesley's Chapel and House and the Museum of Methodism, London; and Englesea Brook Chapel and Museum of Primitive Methodism in Cheshire) as well as to the hundreds of other locations of particular interest to Methodists (about which you can discover more on their website[28]). Surely, though, every church building of whatever denomination has a story, a history, which could be brought alive. Tracing the history of our own tradition is a valid form of pilgrimage, but the past needs to connect with both the present and the future for transformation to take place.

For some, their only conscious engagement with the idea of pilgrimage might be an annual trip to a festival; Greenbelt, Glastonbury, Easter People (and its successor events), Soul Survivor or, for former generations, camp meetings. Some of these have, over the years, changed their location, suggesting that in such cases, it is the gathering of people which is more important than the physical place. I have met many people for whom an annual journey to Cliff College in Derbyshire has been a kind of pilgrimage, from the bank holiday rallies of previous decades to the current "CliffFest" which offers spiritual nourishment and worship.

Church walks: My father ran a church walking club for decades when I was growing up. Admittedly it's probably true that I didn't always want to turn out of bed on the designated Saturday each month and join a group of Methodists to wander in various locations in Shropshire and Staffordshire, but looking back I realize what a valuable activity it was in many ways. Not only did we get fitter and have a good dose of fresh air, not only did we get to know each other better (for there is no better environment than walking side-by-side with someone to facilitate story-sharing), but the group created a safe space for people on the edge of church or Christian faith. Partners, siblings, children and neighbours were invited along by their churchgoing contact and discovered in the open air that these Methodists (even the minister) were relatively

---

[28] http://www.methodistheritage.org.uk/, accessed 10 February 2023.

normal and good company. Husbands in particular seemed to find this an accessible way into the faith of their wives, and I have no doubt that the higher-than-average male-to-female ratio in that church owes much to the monthly walks. They were never billed, nor even conceived, as pilgrimage, but it wouldn't have taken much imagination to turn them into something a little more intentional and thought-provoking (but gently does it, we don't want to spoil the formula with too much religion).

In most of the circuits where my husband Andrew has been stationed, he has initiated some kind of walk around the churches. All Methodists will recognize how easily we become siloed into our own congregations and know little (or, worse, want to know nothing) of our neighbouring Methodists. As mission partners in Grenada, South Caribbean, to mark the year 2000, Andrew suggested a walk which would take in all 12 congregations in the island within a 24-hour period. Not many hours' sleep could be fitted in between seeing in the New Year (widely hailed as a new millennium) and starting out on the road at 5 a.m., but about 12 brave souls were ready for the off. During the day, around 30 more joined for some part of the 30-mile pilgrimage, finishing back in St George's, the capital, after darkness had fallen. Again, it wasn't marketed as a pilgrimage but it certainly had aspects of it, and without doubt it engendered understanding, friendship and reconciliation across the circuit.

Coming to the Strathclyde circuit in 2015 presented a larger challenge—Methodist churches in Scotland are more widely located than in most of England, and the distance around the 12 congregations in the circuit was far too great to be walked in a day. A series of four Saturdays was planned instead, covering different sections of the circuit. I only managed to join one of them, but it sticks in my mind for the depth of conversation and sharing I experienced with people I met for the first time. What stories our landscapes have to tell! And what better way to get to know people in a new area than to walk the landscapes, inviting those who have lived here for years to tell the stories to the incomers.

It doesn't have to be all about churches of course; a stone cross in the centre of a village will have a story; so will an ancient set of stocks, or a folly, or an erratic boulder. Plaques can point us to something to be explored; when walking in London once I came across a sign which read: "The Great Conduit stood in this street providing free water 13th Century to 1666"—what a pilgrimage that could trigger! Unfortunately I took a photo but didn't write down the name of the street, so I will have to walk the streets of London until I find it again! In areas where chapels no longer have a congregation, there may be opportunities to create some sort of pilgrim trail and space for encounter with God; I have seen something of this being explored in some of the most beautiful parts of the Connexion—in Shetland and on the Isle of Man, where the annual "Praying the Keeills" event is very much a community pilgrimage. Other places too have regular parish walks or "beating the bounds"—perhaps an opportunity to share the pilgrim ethos with a wider group.

Pilgrimage can happen anywhere, and I hope to see a lot more of it in Methodism in the coming years. Walks of witness on Palm Sunday, Good Friday, Pentecost or other dates can be designed as pilgrimages, especially when they include times of prayer in significant places, perhaps linking into the "healing on the streets" initiative. Prayer walks too are undertaken in many localities—in groups or individually; these can be extended to become pilgrimage. Perhaps my favourite example came from Sheffield where I heard of a group of women all over the age of entitlement to a bus pass, who spasmodically came together for a "bus pass pilgrimage" using their passes to travel entire bus routes, stopping off for refreshment at any churches or coffee shops on the route and praying for the city as they went!

There are caveats to all this travelling about; firstly, I sense how easy it would be to spend all my spare time going to all these places and ticking them off a list. If I do so, I've lost the plot—pilgrims are more than religious tourists. But balance that risk against discovering the significance of sacred space and it can be transformative. Secondly, when a definite building or location is the destination, it mustn't become more important than the process of the journey. For the pilgrim the travelling is always as much a part of the experience as the arrival.

The second P: People

Many pilgrimages have been devised following in the footsteps of certain people: Jesus, Paul or another biblical character (wouldn't it be something to walk in the footsteps of Ruth from Moab to Bethlehem?!) ... Cuthbert, Aidan, Hilda, Columba, Patrick, Brigid and the many others associated with Celtic spirituality... Wesley (choice here of John, Charles and Susanna—all good material for pilgrimages) ... Cranmer, Asbury, Luther (despite his personal misgivings!).

But again there is a caveat: what are we doing in seeking to follow in someone's footsteps? As Methodists we are not given to venerating saints and martyrs, and we must be attentive to the danger of being sucked into idolatry. Yet one of the joys of exploring pilgrimage over the last ten years has been to learn more about some of these great figures of the past. In preparation for the Lindisfarne pilgrimages, I have read what I can about Aidan and Cuthbert; I have a great affection for them and the gospel they lived and preached, often at huge personal cost. Walking in their footsteps, visiting their graves and seeing their landscapes has given me time and space to ponder on their priorities, and to learn from them as I offer myself to God.

If it's not too self-absorbed, an individual might make a pilgrimage through their own life to observe the grace of God at work. Seizing on the idea of a friend, for my own fiftieth birthday I invited my close family to join me outside the house where I was born and to accompany me around that village, noting my schools, friends' homes, the church where I had become a member and been married and even such places as the bench where one boyfriend finished with me! Such a pilgrimage overlaps with our thinking about "place" and may well include locations where any one of us, like John Wesley in Aldersgate Street, felt our heart strangely warmed.

The third and final P: Purpose

A particularly Methodist take on pilgrimage might be to link it with a particular purpose, such as protest, penitence or politics. So we may consider sites of martyrdom; for example, the burnings of Nicholas Ridley and Hugh Latimer for their Protestant beliefs on 16 October 1555 in Oxford. In Jerusalem, the famous Via Dolorosa marks the traditional route of Jesus' final walk to Calvary and can be undertaken with the purpose of entering into Christ's sufferings. What are the protests of the past which have something to say to the present? How can we use our stories to change the world now? Our Methodist focus on social justice might call to mind the Jarrow march of October 1936 or the fall of the Berlin Wall in November 1989. Two Methodist ministers, Richard Sharples and Simon Topping, have organized a number of pilgrimages to Tolpuddle to highlight and stand in contemporary solidarity with the rights and risks of the Tolpuddle Martyrs. "Green walks" with an environmental focus may be a way of highlighting the climate crisis in which we find ourselves. Again there is no shortage of material, although some research may be needed. Perhaps you can pull together people with specific knowledge or experience; local history groups, other churches, schools, students, political parties, trades unions, campaigners... when that happens, there is another good result.

A brief exercise which could give rise to pilgrimage in a local situation

PLACE:

- Where is your holy place/sacred centre/important site?
- Could that site become part of a pilgrimage?
- If you asked your congregation/group/friends the same question, what might result?

HISTORY/TRADITION:

- What event from history (biblical to last week) grabs your imagination?
- Could that incident give rise to pilgrimage?
- If you asked your congregation/group/friends the same question, what might result?
- What other objects/experiences/happenings could lend themselves to pilgrimage? Art? Music? Birth/death/family story?

FAITH/DOUBT/MISSION:

- What matters most? How do we prioritize? What are we carrying?
- How could pilgrimage help?
- With whom locally could we be in partnership? Ecumenical/inter-faith partners; schools/colleges; rambling/walking groups/local history groups...

The fourth P is not a P: Pilgrimage does not have to be Physical

On many occasions, I have encountered the phenomenon that when the word "pilgrimage" is used people either expect that they have to be physically fit and/or wealthy to take part or they resign themselves to being armchair spectators watching someone else's slides of the Camino ... perish the thought! Pilgrimage is big enough and wild enough to reach anyone in any situation.

Prayer journeys and labyrinths

Many of us will have been involved with setting up or participating in "journeys" around a church (or other) building. Holy Week lends itself to this particularly well, but again there are many resources, possibilities and activities which could be included in such a church event from colouring to walking the labyrinth—a kind of self-contained pilgrimage in its own right. I have experienced myself all the stages of Chapters 6–9 in that simple, short, spiritual walk and walking an outdoor labyrinth lit by candles is a particularly evocative experience. But be warned...

Running a quiet day about pilgrimage once for a group of women with varied levels of physical fitness, I planned to set up a number of rooms for the quiet afternoon sessions, as well as a route for a self-guided walking pilgrimage in the neighbouring streets. The mandala room was fine, the colouring room with Celtic crosses and images based on the Lindisfarne Gospels was fine, the finger labyrinth printed on paper for people to use whilst seated for reflection was fine... but I also wanted to set up a walking labyrinth using rope in the large hall. Andrew and I bought a long length of climbing rope and we practised in the back garden, using what we thought was a relatively simple labyrinth design. Andrew, who had never done this before, but who possessed an excellent mathematical and spatially aware brain, found it immediately intuitive and had it laid out in no time. At this point I fell into one of those traps frequently set for us by pride; if Andrew (with little experience of quiet days or pilgrimage) could do this so easily, it would be no problem for me the next day. I didn't pay enough attention as I merrily coiled the rope and packed it into the car. Next day was quite a different story; with a paper design in one hand and an uncooperative skein of rope in the other I tried and tried to bring the two together... to no avail. Sweating, muttering and humbled I had to scrub that alternative from the day's options but not without learning a lesson or two!

Properly laid out and properly presented, however, a labyrinth can be an accessible form of pilgrimage which has ancient roots. I am grateful to Fiona Fidgin, whose work with the Methodist Church in various roles in recent years has enabled me to see her in action and hear her talk about the history and possibilities of the labyrinth. She explains how, in response to the increasing difficulties in travelling to the Middle East for pilgrimage in the Holy Land, the Roman Catholic Church appointed seven pilgrimage cathedrals to "become" Jerusalem for pilgrims. The labyrinths created at those sites are called the "Chemin de Jerusalem" (the way of Jerusalem) and their centres designated the "New Jerusalem". The idea captured the imagination of many in the Middle Ages and the walls and windows of these Gothic cathedrals were richly decorated to represent the celestial city.

Pilgrim prayer stations

In 2016, I was invited to provide a series of prayer stations for the annual residential Methodist Women in Britain weekend conference. Some notes from these follow and they could be developed in other ways for a pilgrimage focus at a retreat or quiet day. The series consisted of five stations using the aspects of pilgrimage explored in Chapters 6–9; Restlessness and departure; What am I carrying?; The pilgrim way; The sacred centre; Return and re-entry.

1. Restlessness and departure
Visual display includes slippers and walking boots.

Printed material including Stephen Shipley's "restlessness" quotation (see Introduction), prayers or quotations about stepping through the door and questions such as:

- Are you aware of an inner restlessness?
- Is it time to step out of your comfort zone?
- Is your spirit wearing slippers or boots?

Provide a pile of small cards (like train tickets) along with the following instruction:

- On one side write something which you would like to change; on the other side write a fear related to that change. Take the ticket with you as you travel through these prayer stations.

2. What am I carrying?
Visual display includes piles of possible luggage items, e.g. Bible, clothing, umbrella, wallet, rucksack, bum bag, shoes, hairdryer, sweets, water bottle, lunch box, first-aid kit, toiletries, cagoule, waterproof trousers, gloves and hat, books, notebook... along with a cairn of small stones.

Printed material includes the following: "HELP! What do I leave behind?" and these thoughts:

- We all carry baggage—perhaps it is what distinguishes pilgrims from day trippers, but too much baggage slows us down....
- Cards shaped like a ton weight listing possible "baggage" relevant to the situation. The following give ideas of church baggage and emotional baggage: We always do it like this/ We're not that sort of church/ This church will see me out/ Keeping it open but keeping it empty/ We all prefer it like this/ Young people make such a mess/ Fear/ Responsibility/ Hurt/ Unforgiveness/ Anxiety/ Loneliness...
- What is the baggage you need to leave behind? Pick up a stone to symbolize what you are carrying in life and hold it for the remainder of your journey through these prayer stations.

3. The Pilgrim Path
(ideally situated near a window, or outdoors, if possible)

Visual display recreates the Pilgrim Path to Lindisfarne—perhaps with five bamboo poles or (ideally) rounders posts.

Copies of a printed card for each person to take along the "Pilgrim Path" with an instruction for each pole.

1. Rhythm of movement: Breathe deeply, allow your body to take over from your mind, adopt the rhythm of movement.
2. Let Creation speak: Look around you—what are the colours, textures, horizons and details that speak to you?
3. Pilgrims and companions: Others have walked the pilgrim path for many centuries. Be inspired by the saints, including those walking this way today.
4. Which way next? The way ahead is not always obvious, but look ahead to the next pole—what is the next step?
5. Mud: Sometimes the way is difficult—steep or muddy, cold or exposed. Doubts flood in. Was this journey such a good idea after all? Press on.

4. The Sacred Centre
(Preferably an enclosed quiet space—could be in a corner or a circle of chairs—small table in centre. Quiet music if possible; fabric; candles...)

Printed material offers an invitation to sit and be still, meditating on printed images and texts such as:

- Protection: Image of a castle: The LORD is a stronghold for the oppressed, a stronghold in times of trouble. Psalm 9:9
- Watching over: A watch tower: The LORD will keep your going out and your coming in from this time on and for evermore. Psalm 121:8
- Guidance: A road or path: Our heart has not turned back, nor have our steps departed from your way. Psalm 44:18
- Encounter: A wilderness: In the wilderness prepare the way of the LORD, make straight in the desert a highway for our God. Isaiah 40:3
- Prayer: A garden: They went to a place called Gethsemane; and he said to his disciples, "Sit here while I pray." Mark 14:32
- Incarnation: Bethlehem star/a stable/manger: They shall name him Emmanuel, which means, "God is with us.. Matthew 1:23
- Death and resurrection: A tomb: Now there was a garden in the place where he was crucified and in the garden there was a new tomb in which no one had ever been laid. John 19:41
- Provision: Sea of Galilee/picnic: Then Jesus took the loaves, and when he had given thanks, he distributed them to those who were seated; so also the fish, as much as they wanted. John 6:11

5. Return and re-entry—Chairs set out like a bus/train
Printed material: "Soon it will be time to return to 'normal' life. Give yourself a short 'buffer zone' by taking a seat on the re-entry train."
Individual sheets for each pilgrim:

- Pause, give thanks for your pilgrimage and prepare yourself for re-entry...

- Think about someone you will be pleased to see, or who will be pleased to see you when you leave here. Give thanks for that person.
- Name in your thoughts something you are not looking forward to doing when you return home. Ask for courage and grace.
- Think about a situation in the wider world which needs prayer. As you leave this space, leave your stone on the prayer mat of the world as a sign of your prayers for others and your readiness to re-engage with the needs of the world.

Ecumenical and inter-faith pilgrimage

The space and flexibility of pilgrimage makes it a fruitful ground for ecumenical and inter-faith adventures. Christians do not by any means have a monopoly on pilgrimage, although this is the predominant focus of this book. We have much to learn about pilgrimage from our siblings of other faiths, many of whom undertake regular pilgrimages with great devotion. An Anglican vicar, Julian Penfold, married to a Methodist minister, Helen, devised a pilgrim exploration of two churches in the same village which belonged to different denominations. The day brought people together in worship, prayer and journeying and could be adapted for any context.

Sedentary and creative pilgrimage

- Without our moving from a chair, pilgrim verses and images can guide our spirit on a journey. Any creative pastime could be a window into the pilgrim spirit.
- Even walking around a church or a labyrinth is more than some can manage, physically; can they not also be pilgrims? When I shared with MHA chaplains in the retreat mentioned above, we spoke a little of seeing the journey to death as a pilgrimage. Adopting or nurturing some of the pilgrim attitudes and ethos which feature in Chapters 5–9 might indeed make our passage through the final stages of life more purposeful or poignant.
- Edel McClean has done some work on chronic pain in the context of pilgrimage, where getting from your chair to the bathroom may be a very painful and demanding journey.

Pilgrimage resources

A possible act of worship for pilgrims[29]

- *This worship, in seven sections, could be shared as a group or used by an individual; it could take place in a church, in a front room, in a kitchen, or in a garden or field, or on a hillside. It could involve a physical journey, or take place sitting still. Suggested music could be sung or listened to.*
- *To maintain maximum flexibility no guidance is given for allocating the "voices". If you are using this on your own, you may find that there are different voices inside you, some more daring than others! If you are using it as a group, try to avoid the same person always asking/answering the questions—each member of the pilgrim band can encourage others at different times.*

The invitation

- The invitation to come and be a pilgrim is an ancient call. In different ways God summoned Abram and Sarai, Moses and Miriam, Simon and Andrew, Martha and Mary. Today God summons us, "Come and be a pilgrim!"
- What do I need to be a pilgrim?
- You need to feel a little restless, to be wondering if there is more to life, more to God, than you have found so far . . .

Music: a song of invitation e.g. "Come with me, come wander" (*StF* 462) or "Who would true valour see?" (*StF* 486)

---

[29] This was first published in *Magnet* 125 (Summer 2021) and is reproduced with permission.

The preparation

- How do I prepare to come on this pilgrimage? What should I pack into my rucksack?
- It's more a case of what you need to leave behind... don't carry too much or you will become tired and your feet will hurt. Pack a little courage and a sense of adventure, and don't take yourself too seriously.

Prayer:

Journeying God, with excitement and a little trepidation I hear your voice calling me today to set off on a pilgrimage, to travel deeper into you.

Strengthen my weak knees and renew my resolve to stay close to you, whatever twists and turns the journey might involve.

Open my eyes and ears to be attentive to your guiding Spirit. Amen.

The departure

- Ready to set off? Before departing, pause, look over your shoulder—what are you leaving behind to become a pilgrim?
- Everything I've ever known! The security and comfort of what is familiar!
- I'm leaving behind the old me. I need to break away from things which have held me back...

Silence: Keep a few moments of silence to reflect on leaving things behind, whether that is welcome or difficult.

The company

- Am I the only one on this journey?
- Sometimes it will feel as if you are. Sometimes a pilgrim walks alone, quietly reflecting, communing with God, paying attention

to what is around. Even then you are surrounded by the company of saints, those in every age who have responded to the call to be a pilgrim. Sometimes you may want to lean on them.
- Sometimes you will be glad of others around you. You will need them to offer you a hand, a smile, an encouraging word—and sometimes you will need to do the same for them. The pilgrim band is one of the greatest joys of this journey.

Music: "Brother, sister, let me serve you" (*StF* 611) (Verses 1 and 2 could be sung here, verses 3 and 4 after the testimony/pause, and verses 5 and 6 after the prayers).

Testimony: Someone may share a story of needing the help of others along life's journey. Or pause and reflect on those who have pulled you out of the mud over the years.

Prayers: In silence or aloud offer prayers for any you know who are struggling on life's journey at this time.

The path

- I'm worried about getting lost.
- What an amazing view!
- My feet are getting blistered.
- I've never felt so fit!
- I'm hungry.
- I feel closer to God than I ever have before.
- Pilgrimage is wonderful but pilgrimage is also demanding. Just like life, it is a mixture of joy and sorrow, laughter and tears, blessing and pain.
- Sometimes we don't know which path to choose, we may have to sit down and wait, or we may choose the wrong way and need to retrace our steps, hurting our pride as well as our feet.
- Sometimes the terrain holds dangers and difficulties which we hoped never to face in the journey. We will need times of rest, of healing, of refreshment. All pilgrims do.

Read: Luke 9:51–62

Reflection: (Alternatively a longer reflection could be offered by someone present or these ideas could be discussed in groups.)

- Luke tells us that Jesus "set his face to go to Jerusalem". How much did he know—or guess—of what would await him there?
- How tempted was he to turn the other way instead or to hide away in Bethany with good friends who would look after him?
- Perhaps it was his own inner turmoil which led him on to speak challenging words to those would-be followers; "No one who puts a hand to the plough and looks back is fit for the kingdom of God."

Music: "The Lord's my shepherd" (*StF* 481)

Smaller and ranged left

- Does this pilgrimage have a destination in mind?
- That's a good question—some do, some don't. But every pilgrimage has within it a "sacred centre"—an encounter with God.
- You can't predict when that will be, you have to be attentive, open to the whisper of God's Spirit or the crashing of God's waves of love and grace.
- It's the glimpse of glory which makes all the blisters seem unimportant!

Pause: Light a candle, play some special music... give thanks to the God who is present with you, whether at this moment you sense that or not.

The return

- How do you feel now? Are you glad you came?
- I can't put into words how I feel... I am longing for the comfort of home and yet I don't want this to end...

- Everything on this earth ends, but everything is renewed too. The end of every journey is the beginning of the next. Like the voice of prayer, the call to be a pilgrim is never silent.

Music: "Captain of Israel's host" (*StF* 459) or "Have you heard God's voice?" (*StF* 662)

Blessing:

> May God the Path-Maker bless you in all your journeying;
> may Jesus the Pilgrim travel with you every step of the way and
> may the navigating Holy Spirit guide you each day. Amen.

Prayers

Some possible prayer resources follow, beginning with the lines at the start of Chapters 6–9, which are from a prayer I wrote for the *Methodist Prayer Handbook* when it explored the theme of pilgrimage and follow the fourfold shape I find helpful:

> Thanks be to God for the restlessness which urges action and change;
> help me, Holy Spirit, to pay attention to your prompting.
> Thanks be to God for the pilgrim path which lies ahead;
> help me, Jesus Christ, to walk in step with you.
> Thanks be to God for thin places and safe arrivals;
> help me, Holy Spirit, to encounter you afresh.
> Thanks be to God that every journey's end is also a beginning;
> help me, Jesus Christ, to set my face to
> travel onward with you. Amen.

> Christ, who is the way,
> reveal yourself to me today
> and guide each step I take.

Christ, who is the truth,
forgive me when I pretend to be your friend
and fail to love my neighbour.

Christ who is the life,
thank you for companions whose faith enlivens mine
although the road be hard.

This day, may I prove faithful,
press on towards your welcome light
and know your presence in each blessed hour. Amen.[30]

Daily pilgrim prayers

When Andrew and I led a group, mainly from Scotland, to Palestine/Israel in November 2019, basing our itinerary, where possible, on the text of Luke's Gospel, we wrote the following prayers to use morning by morning and evening by evening:

Morning prayer

Pilgrim God, you travel with us,
open our eyes today to your presence.

Pilgrim Jesus, as we walk the streets you walked,
renew our love for you and for all people.

Pilgrim Spirit, fill us with your restless energy,
in the ongoing search for grace and truth.

---

[30] Prayers from the *Methodist Prayer Handbook 2015–16* "Pilgrims on a Journey" © Trustees for Methodist Purposes, reproduced with permission of TMCP and of the authors.

As we continue our pilgrimage today,
may we meet you in unexpected places,
hear you speak in stillness and in clamour,
see your face in those we meet,
share your love with all we encounter,
and draw closer to you step by step.[31]

Evening prayer

Jesus Christ, you have walked the road with us through this day.
**As night falls and the daylight fades, stay with us we pray,
 lodge with us and make yourself known to us.**

We welcome the night, Jesus our Companion, recalling

(one or more of the following sentences may be used)
your birth by night in Bethlehem,
your encounter with Galilean disciples fishing all night,
your nights praying in the hills around Nazareth,
your evening walks from Jerusalem to the Mount of Olives.

The Nunc Dimittis

As we pause in your presence, O Christ:
we give you thanks ...
we offer confession ...
we pray for each other ...
Amen

---

[31] Prayer by Alison Judd.

Other resources

Much fine literature and poetry has been written exploring the subject of pilgrimage and this can help the spirit to travel, even when the body is less mobile. A few suggestions are listed below:

Hymns
The hymns included in the "mini-pilgrimage" in Chapter 4 are listed below, along with their numbers in *Singing the Faith* and, where appropriate, copyright information:

- "Will you come and follow me" (The Summons) *StF* 673 John L. Bell and Graham Maule ©1987.
- "Come with me, come wander" (Sing Hey for the Carpenter) *StF* 462 John L. Bell & Graham Maule ©1987.
- "Jesus Christ is waiting" *StF* 251 John L. Bell and Graham Maule ©1988.
- "Because the Saviour prayed" *StF* 675 John L. Bell ©2002.

All used by permission of Wild Goose Resources Group (WGRG). Iona Community, Glasgow, Scotland. wildgoose.scot.

- "Guide me, O thou great Jehovah" *StF* 465 William Williams (1717–91).
- "O God of Bethel" *StF* 475 Philip Doddridge (1702–51).
- "Brother, sister, let me serve you" *StF* 611 Richard Gillard ©1977 Scripture in Song.
- "Sing for God's glory" *StF* 116 Kathy Galloway © Kathy Galloway. Used by permission.
- "Earth's Creator" *StF* 45 Bernadette Farrell.
- "Have you heard God's voice?" *StF* 662 Jacqueline Jones ©2008.
- "Who would true valour see" *StF* 486 John Bunyan (1628–88).
- "Best of all is God is with us" *StF* 610 by Andrew Pratt ©2008 Stainer & Bell Ltd, London, www.stainer.co.uk. Used by permission. All rights reserved.

- "Food to pilgrims given" *StF* 584 Geon-yong Lee.
- "Now let us from this table rise" *StF* 596 Fred Kaan ©1968 Stainer & Bell Ltd, London, www.stainer.co.uk. Used by permission. All rights reserved.
- "May the road rise up to meet you" *StF* 772 Traditional Irish Blessing.
- "Come, let us anew" *StF* 460 Charles Wesley (1707–88).

Poetry

"Pilgrimages" by R. S. Thomas; "The Pilgrimage" by George Herbert; a prayer written by Sir Walter Raleigh, possibly on the eve of his execution, includes the lines, "Give me my scallop-shell of quiet, my staff of faith to walk upon, my script of joy, immortal diet, my bottle of salvation. My gown of glory, hope's true gauge, and thus I'll take my pilgrimage."

Books

In addition to those already mentioned, I gained wisdom and enjoyment from reading:

- Sheryl Kujawa-Holbrook, *Pilgrimage—The Sacred Art: A journey to the centre of the heart* (where I first encountered the word "liminality"), Skylight Paths Publishing, 2013.
- Sarah Meyrick, *Knowing Anna*, (a novel exploring a group pilgrimage taken in memory of Anna after her death)' Marylebone House, 2016.
- Kate Tristram, *The story of Holy Island: An illustrated history*, Canterbury Press, 2009.
- Phil Cousineau, *The Art of Pilgrimage*, San Francisco: HarperCollins Publishers, 1999.

Weaving

In recent years, I have been privileged to get to know Ruth Sprague, a highly skilled weaver with both textiles and words. (See also Walking the Way: A reflection on pilgrimage using weaves and words © Ruth Sprague 2017 (illuminatetheshadows@yahoo.co.uk). I am delighted that Ruth's whimsical "footprints" grace the cover of this book and her simple yet profound prayer ends Chapter 10.

For a weekend conference, "To be a pilgrim", which I was able to organize and host at Cliff College during my year as Vice-President of the Methodist Conference, I asked Ruth to come and be our "weaver in residence". Her presence and creativity added hugely to the event, as pilgrims sat not just at her feet but also at her loom and were guided in weaving a short stretch of a longer, community piece of art which Ruth later gave me. After the weekend, Ruth shared her own ponderings on how weaving and pilgrimage may walk in step with each other.

Random thoughts: weaving and pilgrimage

Ruth Sprague (April 2018)

Weaving

- Everyone starts in a different place and brings a unique perspective.
- Each section reflects the person who weaves and the life experiences that they bring to the loom.
- People approach the weaving with a preconceived notion of where they are heading. It is the facilitator's job to help them understand that the path is not everything and to encourage reflection and creativity and give permission to experiment with the threads.
- As a facilitator you need to befriend the truth that people might weave in a way and direction that is right for them and not necessarily where and how you had hoped they would weave.
- When you look back at the finished hanging you can see how everyone's unique contributions have enriched the whole weave.
- The finished weave is somewhat chaotic but also somehow perfect.
- There are so many lessons to be learned by looking back but no single section can ever be perfectly replicated; it can only inform our continuing weaving.

Pilgrimage

- Everyone starts in a different place and brings a unique perspective.
- Each section reflects the person who walks and the life experiences that they bring to the journey.
- People approach the pilgrimage with a preconceived notion of where they are heading. It is the facilitator's job to help them understand that the path is not everything and to encourage reflection and creativity and give permission to experiment with the journeying.
- As a facilitator you need to befriend the truth that people might undertake a pilgrimage in a way and direction that is right for them and not necessarily where and how you had hoped they would journey.
- When you look back at the finished walk you can see how everyone's unique contributions have enriched the whole pilgrimage.
- The finished walk is somewhat chaotic but also somehow perfect.
- There are so many lessons to be learned by looking back but no single section can ever be perfectly replicated, it can only inform our continuing journey.

Printed by BoD"in Norderstedt, Germany